Politically
Speaking

Judy & Kiké
Rebick & Roach

Politically Speaking

For Gordon
In Solidarity especially
around Quebec
Judy March

Douglas & McIntyre
Vancouver/Toronto

Douglas & McIntyre
1615 Venables Street
Vancouver, British Columbia
V5L 2H1

Canadian Cataloguing in Publication Data

Rebick, Judy.
Politically speaking.

ISBN 1-55054-515-9

1. Canada—Social policy. 2. Feminism—Canada. 3. Canada—
Politics and government—1984–1993* 4. Canada—Politics and
government—1993–* I. Roach, Kiké, 1970– II. Title.
HQ1453.R42 1996   361.6'1'0971   C96-910438-3

Editing by Barbara Pulling
Cover design by Peggy Heath
Cover photograph by Evan Dion
Text design and typesetting by Val Speidel
Printed and bound in Canada by Imprimerie Gagné Ltée
Printed on acid-free paper ∞

The publisher gratefully acknowledges the assistance of the Canada Council
and of the British Columbia Ministry of Tourism, Small Business and Culture.

To the memory of Audre Lorde

"Tomorrow belongs to those of us who conceive of it
as belonging to everyone."

—*A Burst of Light*

CONTENTS

Politically
Speaking

Judy Rebick

STILL CRAZY AFTER ALL THESE YEARS

In his poetic book *The History of the Russian Revolution*, Leon Trotsky uses the metaphor of a rotating stage. As the stage turns, the czar, his brutal Cossacks and their enslaved serfs disappear as the energetic, idealistic working class emerges, arm in arm, from the darkness into the bright theatre lights. Only one change in my life has been that monumental: the rising of women. I remember the day that I decided I would be my own person. I was eight years old, and my mother told me that we were moving to Toronto from Brooklyn, New York. I didn't want to go, and I knew she didn't. Her family, our extended family, were in Brooklyn. My father's family were in Toronto, but they were strangers, even to him. I begged her to convince him not to go. She explained, it is the husband who makes the decisions, and a good wife follows the decisions of her husband. My grandmother back in Brooklyn died one year later, and I knew it was because I wasn't there to take care of her.

I have been a feminist since that day, but I didn't get involved in the women's movement until 1980. I'm glad now that we moved to Canada, which doesn't mean that I've changed my mind about the patriarchy. My politics developed in response to others' suffering, not my own. The anti–Vietnam war movement, the civil rights movement, inspired me more than the women's movement in those early days. A trip around the world when I was twenty-three set me on my path. I travelled alone from Turkey to India on buses. The extreme poverty I saw affected me most deeply on an intellectual level, and the violence and sexual aggression I experienced affected me most deeply psychologically. In Delhi, alone with a high fever and shitting water in 140°F heat, I decided that if I lived I would dedicate the rest of my life to changing the world. Even then I had a gift for hyperbole.

That was more than twenty-five years ago, and I am still trying to change the world. Why have I continued my activism when so many like me have given in, given out or given up? I have had the experience of deciding to fight an injustice and seeing it corrected; of seeing the world change in profound ways because of the organizing and solidarity of people without power; and of watching someone who is hurt and isolated find joy and strength by working with others in common cause. If I began my activism out of anger and confusion about injustice, I continue because it gives me sustenance.

Two years ago, as I was just beginning my stint as the left-wing host on CBC Newsworld's *Face Off*, Barbara Pulling, an editor at Douglas & McIntyre, approached me to write a book on new strategies for the Left. I didn't think it was time yet for such a book. New strategies for the Left are emerging out of the struggles of people around the world. The old projects of the Left, social democracy and communism, have failed to bring us the just society we all envisioned. They, like the capitalism they sought to

reform or overturn, are stuck in patriarchal, elitist power structures. The social movements, especially the women's movement,
arose to overturn the domination of the elites and find a way to an
egalitarian, truly democratic society. The old Left theory was
imposed from the top. The new Left theory is emerging from the
bottom.

A few days after my meeting with Barbara, Kiké Roach, a
young woman I had known since she showed up one year as a
teen-ager at an annual general meeting of NAC, the National
Action Committee on the Status of Women, expressed her frustration that none of the books by feminists talked about politics.
They were all in the realm of ideas. Nothing she could read told
her about how the women's movement had organized to achieve
the monumental changes of the last thirty years. I asked her if she
wanted to write a book together, and *Politically Speaking* is the
result. I hope it will contribute to developing the new theory and
strategy we need for the days and years ahead.

I wanted to work with Kiké because I believe that the women's
movement has not paid enough attention to the needs and voices
of young women. Originally, I conceived the book as a dialogue
between a young activist and a long-term, experienced activist.
What has emerged is much more a cross-race dialogue than a
cross-generational one. For anyone who thinks that race is not a
central determinant in how we are treated in the world and therefore how we experience it, I hope this book will dispel that illu-
sion. No matter what the topic, from Quebec to political parties,
Kiké's understanding as a Black woman emerges as central to her
vision. Originally she resisted the cross-generational aspect of the
dialogue. Fed up with the nonsense about Generation X, she
fought my stereotypes about her age group, and that too forms
part of our dialogue. She wanted me to talk about being Jewish,
and I resisted that. Being Jewish, I thought, had very little to do

with my political identity. But through our conversations I realized that maybe it has had more of an influence than I admitted.

From the moment I got involved in anti-racist activism, I've been frustrated by how little the media or most white people understand about racism. Every struggle by women of colour to be heard has been reflected through the distorting prism of the media. While the work of white American feminists like Gloria Steinem and Naomi Wolf or anti-feminists like Camille Paglia and Christina Hoff Sommers receives wide attention in Canada, books of enormous wisdom written by Black feminists like Audre Lorde and bell hooks are available only to those who know about them. The insistence of so many that racism is really just the purview of a few neo-Nazis and has nothing to do with us nice, liberal-minded white folk is extraordinary. A friend of mine who travels the world said to me that when he is told a society is not racist, he checks it out by riding the subway, at 6:00 a.m., 7:00 a.m., 8:00 a.m. and 9:00 a.m. What he invariably finds is that the earlier the hour, the more people of colour who are passengers. In Canada it is easier than that. Just look at the House of Commons, any newsroom in the country or any place of power, like the stock exchange or academia, and then ride the subway, go to a suburban mall. Where are the people of colour?

I have learned in the women's movement that anti-racism is not just about inclusion; it is about ending the domination of elites. Women's equality is meaningless if it is only equality for white, middle-class women. And just as men can't give equality to women—we have to take it—so white women cannot give equality to women of colour. Why it is so difficult for white women who have fought a lifetime against oppression to understand this point is beyond me. I hope our book will help them to understand, and maybe help to heal some of the hurt. And I hope that our dialogues will provide a window to those outside the women's movement on what I believe is a historical struggle for equality that has been more successful in the Canadian women's movement than anywhere else in the world. A lot of leadership now comes from the communities of colour in our country, and will continue to do so. The process of transformation from a white supremacist to a truly multicultural and multiracial society must be an essential part of the socialist and feminist political project.

But this book is about more than racism. When Kiké and I began our dialogue in the spring of 1995, everything looked very bleak for progressive people in Canada. Hopes that defeating the Mulroney Tories federally would mean defeating a right-wing agenda were dashed. Neo-conservative economic policies seemed to have captured the entire political landscape. Dissenting voices were completely silenced. Mike Harris and his right-wing counterrevolutionaries were about to take power in Ontario, and the Left was divided and demoralized by the betrayals of NDP government under Bob Rae. I spent every night on my TV show debating right-wingers, often about economic policies. It was as if I was the only voice on the Left still being heard. I felt isolated and impotent for the first time in many years. Talking politics with Kiké helped me to put that desperately low moment into perspective. Movements for social change have ebbs and flows. Our flow began in the late 1960s. It continued in Canada much longer than in many other places, until the early 1990s. Then we ebbed big-time. Low tide for leftists. Now I feel the tide is slowly starting to come in again.

Our dialogues are part of the new tide of social change that will soon sweep the world. I saw it forming in Bejiing during the UN Women's Conference; on the streets of Germany, France and Hamilton, Ontario; in Quebec and across Canada during the Women's March against Poverty; in the mountains of Mexico and the barrios of Brazil. We *will* find a new model for socialism, one that brings together all the wisdom and experience of generations of struggle, and all the energy and creativity of those who have been shunted to the margins of history.

Kiké Roach

WHY I SPEAK

In 1979, two white cops killed a Black man named Albert Johnson. After months of harassing him, they killed him in his own home, in front of his seven-year-old daughter. I was nine at the time, and I remember going to the house where it all happened, seeing the shattered door frame where the police had busted in, the blood stains splattered on the kitchen wall. I remember trying to put into words how I felt as I held my own father's hand and we approached the casket to view Albert Johnson's body. It was my first encounter with death and my first lesson in what injustice looks like, in what it feels like. My family joined with hundreds of others pouring out onto the streets of Toronto to protest police brutality, and it was walking with the community that gave me a sense of the power we have as people, people who care about life, about justice.

I've been demonstrating ever since.

Brian Mulroney, Ronald Reagan and Maggie Thatcher loomed large over my growing up. Reading through my old diary, I see that the anxiety I felt as a teen-ager had not so much to do with what my friends thought of me as with my fear that the world might blow up at any moment. In the early eighties, nuclear annihilation seemed like a real possibility. Reagan was calling the Soviet Union the "evil empire," and Dr. Helen Caldicott was explaining in graphic detail what the world would look like the day after the big one dropped. Meanwhile, what looked like a nuclear holocaust seemed to have already hit parts of Ethiopia, as TV flashed images of starving people into our living rooms. For some of us, the Day After was now.

Today the Right has found a new evil empire to attack—the welfare state. And in the whirl of slash and burn, deficit politics attacks equality through the back door. Calling on fear-mongering and hatred, the powers that be encourage us to betray the vision of a just society for all. Betrayal's name is backlash. And the faces of its targets are familiar: immigrants, women, the poor, and young Blacks in particular, who are still economically useful to a justice system that thrives on jailing us in ever higher numbers.

My consciousness was formed through involvement in the struggle to stop the deportation of Jamaican women domestic workers, through the anti-apartheid movement, the Montreal massacre. It was formed through seeing the Canadian military tanks at Oka turned on the Kahnienkehaka (Mohawk) people who defended their sacred burial grounds against settlers' plans for a golf course. I woke up walking past the downtown Toronto ruins where an abortion clinic stood before it was bombed, vestiges of violence from right-to-lifers. My consciousness was moulded from long nights reading Angela Davis and Audre Lorde and spending a day in jail for civil disobedience.

But it is my family, by far, who have most influenced my thinking and actions. Each of us daughters has worked in the family law firm that has fought civil rights cases for thirty years. There have been so many community meetings at our house that we don't even bother to take down the "No Smoking, Please" signs any more. Progressive lawyers, educators, artists and activists from all over the world have come to stay. And it's hard to ignore their stories or resist wanting to follow in their footsteps.

At our house there is always talk of politics, so it seemed only natural for me to say yes when Judy Rebick asked me if I wanted to do this book with her. When we met for brunch that first Sunday, I was hungry for more than just pancakes. I wanted to talk about what is happening to progressive people in these times. I wondered how she felt, after years of organizing, about what is going on today. Over the year we met, a lot of incredible things happened. It was the year of the sensational Paul Bernardo and O. J. Simpson trials; of Mike Harris sweeping to power in Ontario on a right-wing campaign of scapegoating and division; of the country almost coming apart on referendum night.

I was seventeen and making placards saying "Women Will Be Heard" when I first met Judy at a NAC annual general meeting. I have to admit that if it weren't for the many women who fought for years to make NAC more democratic, representative and "real," I might never have returned, let alone served on NAC's board. Organizing Freedomrides and mass demonstrations, lobbying or heckling politicians, fighting for immigrants' rights and against job discrimination, I'e confronted the system. But through talking with Judy I've realized that it is sometimes *just as* important to work for change *inside* the organizations that are supposed to represent us.

When it comes to issues of cultural representation, Judy and I diverge. But our discussions showed me that sometimes you can be an ally to another group even when you hold a different opinion. Privilege need not be a barrier to understanding or a liability when we work to end it by sharing power. Judy and I have found common cause despite different life experiences, and it's on the basis of a shared passion for social justice that we can work together.

Having the luxury to speak out in a world where so many battle just to survive is a precious gift. Speaking for equality and justice for all is the only way I know to honour it. I come from people who were enslaved and stripped of everything. From resilient people who have known every injustice and still come out fighting. I come from people who know Canada as a place where people search and struggle and create new identities. My Canada includes callaloo and roti, Caribana, reggae and resistance. I draw on Caribbean, American, African and Canadian traditions. And I know that no matter how bad things seem, we've seen worse, but always we overcome. Strong talk and rock-hard determination have seen us through. Faith has kept us here and, with each step forward, "is freedom we makin'."

Contrary to media mythology, feminism and the Left do have answers. We've been offering them throughout human history. Today we need to do that more and better. The Right has made gains in part because our opposition has not been as vocal or as visible as it needs to be. In these times of increasing insecurity, polarization and anger, we need every voice to help create a tomorrow that belongs to all of us. As Westerners, we must reexamine our whole way of living. As progressives, we must scrutinize our practices, mobilize our base and articulate our agenda. To paraphrase Martin Luther King Jr., the challenge for the Left is to discover how to transform our considerable strengths into a lasting power.

I hope too that our dialogues help to dispel some myths. People of my age have been branded "Generation X" and accused of apathy and indifference. But our realities, anxieties and accomplish-ments cannot be summarized or symbolized by a letter in the alphabet. Activism is not unique to any generation. It is not the property of the sixties, although there are a lot of important lessons to be drawn from that time. Progressive young people *do* exist, and there is still reason for us to organize. I'm inspired by the students across Canada who've walked out to protest higher tuition and deteriorating services; by the youth who rebelled against apartheid during the Soweto uprisings; by twelve-year-old Iqbal Masih, who escaped modern-day slavery and crusaded against child labour; by the fifteen-year-old girl who wrote to me while I was a NAC executive member saying that she knew women before her had broken down barriers to make her life bet-ter. And she didn't want to sit around; she wanted it to be her turn. She said, "I want to fight."

A woman from Chad once told me that there is a plant in Africa that takes twenty-five years before it flowers, but its roots are deep, and when it finally matures, its medicinal properties have powerful healing qualities. The hope I have for this generation, and those to come, is the hope for deep roots and the power to heal.

1

Hitting Hard, Hitting Fast

. . . .

THE NEW RIGHT

JUDY REBICK: Cataclysmic changes are happening around the world. The impact of globalization has been enormous: free trade, downward pressure on wages and working conditions, a push for privatization and deregulation, high levels of unemployment and the erosion of social programs. The decline in living standards for most people has been pretty devastating. People are also feeling an extraordinary lack of control over their lives, much more than ever before.

KIKÉ ROACH: I hate this notion that the New Right agenda is "revolutionary" and coming up with all these fresh new ideas, when in fact it is just the opposite. They are taking the same old, tired ideas we have seen over thousands of years and repackaging them. But their policies amount to the same thing: handing power over to a tiny elite group of super-rich men who lord it over the rest of us.

JR: That's why the term "neo-liberalism" is used. The ideology we hear from everyone from federal Finance Minister Paul Martin to Reform Party leader Preston Manning is nineteenth-century liberalism, which was based on unfettered, free-market capitalism—or, as Pierre Elliott Trudeau called it, "savage capitalism."

There is worldwide pressure on governments from business and international investment markets to move to the right. Corporate power is much greater, much more concentrated and much more mobile than in the past. I think there are a number of reasons for this. The collapse of the Communist bloc has opened up vast new markets and reduced the limits of capitalist expansion, as well as removing the Communist threat, which I think did keep attacks against workers partly in check. The technological revolution permits incredible mobility of capital and production as well as reducing the need for a trained work force, and capital is intensely unstable now because the means exist to send trillions of dollars zipping around the globe at the push of a button.

Society is being reorganized for the benefit of investors. There are companies that make bigger profits than ever before but still lay off workers. They need to provide a higher return on investment to be competitive. It is shortsighted, of course, because massive layoffs mean workers don't have the money to buy the products or services companies produce. But capitalists have never been known for their foresight.

KR: The international money markets can bring a nation to its knees by deciding for whatever reason that that country's currency is worth half of what it was the other day. The Mexican peso's worth dropped almost overnight, to use just one example.

Money was originally created as a symbol of exchange between people, and now it's being used as a weapon against us. It's incredible that in a lot of countries, like South Africa, for example, you have 30 to 40 per cent unemployment, and yet there are students who want to learn, teachers who want to teach—and that's true here, too. People need food, they need clothing, they need some kind of meaningful work in their lives. That's what's real. But we've made money a commodity.

If you create two pools of workers, one well-paid and another hungry and desperate, a polarization of interests happens that threatens whatever gains the unionized workers have made. When NAFTA, the North American Free Trade Agreement, was being negotiated, there was a lot of opportunity for us to start understanding that sort of dynamic. Some people did see that links with Mexican workers were essential. They argued that we should raise the standard of living of Mexican workers and of non-unionized workers in all three countries by stressing a shorter work week, national health care and a higher minimum wage across the continent. A trade agreement made in the interests of the majority would bring *up* the standard of living of the poorest partner, not bring down the standard of living of the richest.

But instead, our trade agreements are being made only in the interests of corporate profit. Within two years of Canada signing the Free Trade Agreement with the U.S., we lost more than 400,000 manufacturing jobs in Ontario alone. But even though voters got rid of the Tories in the 1993 federal election, the Right has grown stronger in Canada. They tell us that the marketplace can take care of all our needs. All we have to do is be "globally competitive." And to be globally competitive, business says they need fewer regulations. They need less government and lower taxes. But taxes support social programs, and regulations do things like make sure that companies aren't allowed to just ride roughshod on the environment. So "competitive" to me is a code word for eroding people's rights and standard of living.

We've been convinced to accept the idea that the debt and

deficit are our major problems in this country, and if only we could deal with them, things would get better. Or if the government would just create more jobs. But it's much bigger than that. We thought the Liberal Party might be the answer, but then they turned around and signed the NAFTA. When they signed that deal, in a lot of ways we lost our sovereignty. Now, if the federal government wants to protect jobs in Canada by giving Canadian companies subsidies, U.S.-based corporations can challenge that by calling it unfair advantage. What's happened is that we've moved to a new form of government at an international level— government by corporations. And in North America, NAFTA is their constitution. Globalization is just a nicer word for more corporate power.

At the international level we've been seeing a different version of the same story for years. The International Monetary Fund and the World Bank have forced many countries in Africa, Asia and Latin America to adopt austerity measures called "Structural Adjustment Programs." SAPs basically force governments to reorganize their economies so that foreign businesses find it more attractive to operate there. The very rich in these countries benefit, but the poor get poorer, and of course the worst impact is on women, because they have the least resources but the most responsibility for looking after the family.

JR: In 1995 there was a Non-Governmental Organizations Forum in Huairou, China, held in conjunction with the Fourth United Nations Conference on Women in Beijing. Women there made a similar point. Today the issues for people in the North, the mostly wealthy northern nations, and in the South, the mostly underdeveloped, poor nations, are coming much closer together. We've got a lot of the same problems showing up in different ways, although of course we don't suffer anything like people in the South suffer. We often think of globalization as reducing the role of government, but many speakers in Huairou pointed out that what they call neo-liberalism and we call neo-conservatism actually increases the coercive role of the state, and the role of the state in ensuring the most unencumbered movement of capital.

The impact of globalization on the South was best summed up by Gita Sen, who was at the conference representing an international group called DAWN, Development Alternatives for Women in a New Era. As she pointed out, governments that can no longer provide even minimal health and education are maintaining huge arsenals. So the struggle for women's equality today has to focus on challenging the negative economic forces unleashed by globalization and on transforming international institutions and states to be more accountable, as well as building women's groups, unions and people's organizations.

Let's talk about some of the main arguments of the Right in Canada and why they have gained so much ground. The first argument, and the one I think they've been most successful in putting forward, is that we can't afford social programs. This is combined with messages about how social programs create dependency. The Right used to argue that lavish social spending had caused the deficit. But Linda McQuaig, in her book *Shooting the Hippo*, and other economic analysts have shown that high interest rates and high unemployment, not social spending, are the primary culprits for ballooning deficit and debt.

KR: Statistics Canada figures show that less than 10 per cent of the debt comes from spending on social programs.

JR: Nevertheless, the Right says, since we can't control interest rates, our only option is to downsize government and cut social programs. This is the famous "There is no alternative" argument.

The Left has been very slow to develop a credible argument against this position. The best the political Left has done is to cut more humanely, like in Saskatchewan, where the budget cuts have been less focussed on hitting the poor than in other provinces. Those to the left of the NDP argued up to about two years ago that the deficit was just an excuse being used by the corporate sector to justify slashing social programs. It's true that cutting social programs makes the work force more vulnerable. But as we recognize now, the deficit *is* a problem. When a country spends thirty cents on the dollar to pay interest on the debt, there is a problem. The Left should actually be as concerned about this as the Right, since our tax dollars are being used to pay interest to investors, who tend to be in higher income brackets.

KR: The debt and the deficit are problems, but they're problems of the Right's creation. If the government wanted to eliminate the deficit, it could do that without touching social programs. It could start collecting on the $40 billion in deferred taxes owed by big business. So it's not really about the deficit or the debt. If it were, you wouldn't see politicians like Ontario Premier Mike Harris promising a 30 per cent personal income tax cut. I don't think we should play the game of accepting that ordinary people are responsible for this debt.

JR: I agree that we shouldn't blame the poor, the unemployed or public sector workers for the debt, but it is not as simple to solve as you suggest. The Left is just beginning to develop alternate strategies that rely on job creation, tax reform and redefining the mandate of the Bank of Canada to include unemployment, not just inflation. The idea of a tax on capital implemented at the international level—like the Tobin tax, which would tax all financial transactions at a low rate to slow down capital mobility—is also important.

The Right's second major argument is "Government should do only what government can do," to quote Paul Martin. Neo cons argue that everything government does is insufficient. If we want efficiency, they say, we should look to the private sector to run things. There is no evidence for this argument, but it has been made so many times that people start to believe it. Somehow there is a separation made between the quality of public services, which most Canadians value, and the work of public sector workers. This attack on the public sector also prepares the ground for an acceptance of privatization, even in areas where public support is strong, like education. A concerted attack on the quality of public education, based mostly on disinformation, has created a climate in which privatization can sneak in by the back door, for example in the case of charter schools.

KR: In fact, the Right doesn't seem to see much of a role for government at all, aside from privatizing everything in sight. There are so many examples. The CBC is contracting out. Hospitals are turning lab work over to private companies. In Alberta, there are more than a dozen private health clinics, and the Ministry of Economic Development and Tourism there is now managed by a board of businesspeople. Alberta has privatized liquor sales, too. Supposedly to save money, the Liberals in New Brunswick chose a private American company called Wackenhut Corp. to build and manage a jail for young offenders in Miramichi. Apparently crime *does* pay.

When the Right isn't privatizing things, they're thinking of what else they can cut back on. The cuts are probably scariest in the area of health care, because we're talking life and death situations. In Ontario and Alberta, they're trying to get rid of a lot of registered nurses, who go through three years of training, so they can replace them with "patient hostesses," who do an eight- to twelve-week course and will get paid far less. And hospitals are sending patients home faster.

JR: The neo-cons want to download government responsibility for social services onto the community and the family. We often talk about how birth control or human rights codes have helped women, but not about how the welfare state and social programs have contributed. But what are social programs except the state providing for people in a way that only the family and the church used to? Women in the family setting took care of the sick. Women educated children before there were schools. Women stayed home to take care of the kids. So the development of the welfare state was very much a precondition to women's equality. The attacks today on the idea that the state should provide support services like health care, education, welfare and care of the elderly mean that these tasks are falling back to individual women.

Neo-cons are also attacking the gains of the women's movement on equality rights. They say they are for equality, but of course what they mean is the original civil rights notion of equality, which is simply non-discrimination. According to them, systemic discrimination doesn't exist. They argue that individuals who discriminate should be punished but that we don't need positive action like employment equity or pay equity to achieve equality. This is the argument the Reform Party made against including sexual orientation in the federal human rights code. To some it may be incomprehensible that people on the Right think adding the words "sexual orientation" to the code creates special rights for gays and lesbians, until you understand that they don't want *anyone* on that list.

KR: I think it's important for people to know that the Reform Party is against Canada's Charter of Rights and Freedoms. Too often the media portray Reform's problem as the fact that it has bigots in the party, without ever looking at the policies that are attracting these bigots in the first place. Preston Manning only agonizes over public expressions of racism, not racism itself. If we lose focus on the principles and the policies, we get fooled.

Look at the Liberals. They brought in the hate crimes bill, but they have also brought in some of the most regressive immigration laws we've seen in years. The laws are hurting people of colour, who are now the majority of immigrants and refugees coming to Canada because they are fleeing wars and extreme poverty in the South.

The Liberals were under a lot of pressure from the Reform Party to restrict immigration to Canada. But the government took the politics of scapegoating to new heights in 1994. When two Toronto crimes were sensationalized by the media—the Just Desserts incident, in which a Black man is charged with killing a white woman during a robbery attempt, and the killing of a white cop by a Black man—the government used them as justification to clamp down on immigration. Both incidents involved suspects who had lived in Canada for most of their lives but had been ordered deported. Pretty soon we started to hear the federal government talking about how they needed to get tough about deporting immigrants who were criminals. So day after day we heard the words "immigrant" and "criminal" side by side.

Sergio Marchi, who was federal immigration minister at the time, kept reinforcing in the public mind a link between immigration and criminality. Then he brought in changes to further limit family-class immigration, which meant that thousands fewer people were able to come to Canada. Marchi also created a closer relationship between the R.C.M.P. and the immigration department, so that the two could work together to root out these so-called immigrant criminals. As a result, a lot of people of colour, especially people from Jamaica and Somalia, are now experiencing discrimination that really is above and beyond the norm. For example, there are a lot of Jamaican women who have lived here for decades but haven't taken out citizenship. Now their Canadian-born children are being denied benefits. The immigration minis-ter is considering for the first time whether Canadian-born children will automatically get citizenship. I've never seen so many people punished for the deeds of just two. *All* immigrants are being treated like they're criminals. They're being scrutinized in a new way, and wild allegations are being made about them. New refugees are all being portrayed as bilking the welfare system.

JR: Restrictive immigration laws are a way of blaming "the other." When there's high unemployment, you blame immigrants for taking jobs. It happens very subtly in Canada. Nobody openly says that. But when Mike Harris attacks the "quota law," his name for the Ontario Employment Equity Act, I think what he's really saying is that we don't want people of colour taking our jobs. When the federal government imposes a head tax on immigrants, it's a way of suggesting that immigrants are abusing social services.

KR: But the *Toronto Star* reported last year that the average immigrant household pays more in taxes than it takes out in public services. The proceeds from the head tax are not even going into settlement programs. They're just going into general revenue.

The federal Liberals are getting away with far more right-wing policies than the Mulroney government gave us. The Liberals seem to have better public relations consultants than the

Tories did, because they're still popular even though they've made it much harder for anyone to get unemployment insurance, they're chopping billions in transfer payments to the provinces and they seem to have no clear strategy on Quebec or Native issues. But they pulled off the biggest and most undemocratic move in the cleverest way. Paul Martin used his 1995 budget to redesign the fundamental role of federal government by shifting a lot of its powers over social programs to the provinces. When they put all funding for health, education and social assistance into the Canada Health and Social Transfer and repealed CAP, the Canada Assistance Plan, which provided some minimal standards for social assistance, they basically kissed their responsibility to ensure national standards good-bye. And they did it with no mandate from the people. Canadians rejected the devolution of power to the provinces when they voted against the Charlottetown Accord.

JR: Yes, it is amazing how much the Liberals are getting away with. Part of it is that they're so damn smart, and part of it is that as more and more power is devolved to the provinces, the most visible cuts are being made at the provincial level. And unfortunately, although it took ten years, the Right has managed to convince a lot of people that these cuts are necessary. So Paul Martin is able to slash and burn at the same time he claims he's protecting social programs from the barbarian hordes in the Reform Party.

I think one reason right-wing ideology has gained so much ground in North America is that so many things have changed so fast. There have been changes in the economy; changes in the demographics, with the influx of immigrants of colour; changes in the attitudes of citizens to the state, and of children towards their parents; and changes in the patriarchal family, partly as a result of what the women's movement has achieved. For middle- and working-class people, the world as we know it is disintegrating. Expectations of owning a house and having job security have dwindled. Expectations that our children will do better than we did are also mostly gone. People are working harder and having less to show for it.

KR: But the other reason the Right is gaining is because they are using divide-and-conquer tactics successfully. They want to channel people's frustration into a resentment of the wasteful bureaucracy of "big government" and the special interests of "big labour" and the so-called abuse of welfare. In the olden days, the ruling class used a warrior class to protect them; now they just control people with an effective repetition of lies. The Left needs to debunk these lies as well as responding to people's feelings of powerlessness.

JR: Many women who spoke at the NGO conference in Huairou felt that the rise of the religious Right or the social Right is a response to the dislocation of cultural and spiritual values caused by globalization. In many countries, fundamentalists have moved into the gap. Here, groups like the Reform Party respond to people's desire to have more control over their lives and a clear set of values. But their answer is to go backwards instead of moving forward. You've talked about the strong undercurrent of racism in the politics of the New Right. There's a strong strain of sexism, too. The attacks on the poor are sexist; even if the Canadian Right isn't as explicit as Americans are about attacking single mothers, that's what they are doing. And of course the relationship between homophobia and the reinforcement of the traditional nuclear family is obvious. David Frum, probably the most right-wing of all the New Right ideologues in Canada, wrote an article in *Saturday*

Night arguing that Canada's most important and urgent social problem is the strengthening of the traditional family. And the Winds of Change conference, a meeting of New Right elites in Calgary in spring 1996, called for government policy to strengthen the "natural" family.

Clearly, in addition to economic alternatives, the Left and social movements need to speak to this sense of social dislocation. In the women's movement, we long ago abandoned debates about personal relationships. Take the family, for example. When I was younger, my position was that the nuclear family was oppressive to women and we should get rid of it. Then we tried to live in communes, and it was all very idealistic and it didn't work for most people. Now no one talks about getting rid of the nuclear family. But how do we have a more egalitarian one?

KR: We shouldn't abandon the debate about "family values" to the Right. We can learn a lot from cultures where the idea of community is much stronger. Women in the South, who have been living under harsher conditions, have developed some effective ways of dealing with severe economic hardship and with being attacked. In African, Asian and Latin American cultures, there is a very different notion of family. Family is an extended, intricate model of who you are responsible for, who is responsible for you. There is a greater reliance on community and the development of community because people see themselves as interconnected.

In North America, families are changing rapidly. We see more and more different kinds of households being set up, sometimes out of economic necessity. The gay and lesbian community has developed the idea of extended family by including close friends and ex-partners in the definition. But still too many single mothers are struggling without much community support. The cult of individualism and the self in this part of the world is a major weakness. How can we come up with a new model? How can we counteract the Right when everyone drives to work, comes back home and watches television?

JR: If you look at a similar period of dramatic change in history, the Industrial Revolution, you see a polarization in society, with the rise of both a traditionalist right-wing solution and of revolutionary left-wing solutions. What troubles me now, particularly in the North, is that I don't see the development of a new Left in the broadest sense. I think one place where we can learn from the radical Right is that they go to the people.

KR: But in fact they learned this from us. What is new about them is how much they have picked up from us. They have learned from our struggles, learned to market their ideas in a better way. The Right co-opted the issue of the tax burden on the middle and working classes. And by positioning themselves on the side of ordinary people, they gave themselves a new way to gut government services but still look progressive and concerned. We need to connect the taxation crisis back to bad policy decisions. When free trade was instituted, the federal government lost $2 billion because corporations no longer had to pay tariffs. Mulroney stuck us with the GST to make up the shortfall.

Preston Manning realized that there was total dissatisfaction among people who felt that they weren't being heard, that politicians weren't being accountable. He responded by coming up with "populist" strategies, proposing things like people being able to recall their elected officials.

JR: I agree with a lot of Reform's proposals about direct democracy. I think more accountability of politicians and more public debate, including referendums, would be an important advance for democracy. During the Charlottetown Accord debate and the Quebec referendum on sovereignty, I saw more interest in politics in this country than I have ever seen before. When citizens actually have the responsibility to make a decision, they take it very seriously. I believe that major new initiatives, like free trade, like the GST, *should* be put to a referendum after a democratic debate. I think referendums on every little issue undermine the democratic process, since most people don't have time to participate, but occasional referendums on issues of major national importance will enhance democracy. And I think a truly democratic society will be progressive.

The Right often claims that the Liberals and the Left have ruined this country. They've created a myth that left-of-centre governments are responsible for debt, when in fact some right-wing governments, like Devine's in Saskatchewan, had the highest debt of all. I get letters saying, "People like Judy have been running the country long enough." It's crazy. Was Mulroney a leftist? But what is true is that the Left, equality-seeking movements in particular, have managed to define a lot of the issues over the years. In the environmental and anti-racism movements, the women's movement, the gay and lesbian rights movement, we have been setting the agenda in the sense that governments have had to respond to our demands. Not the economic agenda, which has always been defined by the business community, but the social agenda.

KR: We were shaping the public discourse. The eighties were the time of Mulroney, Thatcher and Reagan. But we also had dynamic worldwide movements against apartheid and nuclear armament. Grenada and Nicaragua had socialist revolutions. Women of colour worldwide began generating a lot of powerful feminist theory and recording women's history. And environmental activists put pressure on big companies to stop clearcutting forests. Canadian women won equality rights in the charter and choice on abortion.

JR: Yes. We managed to stand our ground to a certain extent during the Mulroney years, except that we lost the big fight on free trade. Now we have to regroup. This is a different political period. We are not in the ascendancy any more, so how do we reorganize?

KR: The "Hit 'em hard, hit 'em fast and don't blink" approach to massive social change is the Right's most effective strategy. There's so little time to meet, discuss and educate ourselves, let alone to organize a response and a fightback. In Alberta the government targeted the most vulnerable people, and the "I'm not on welfare. Get a job!" crowd sat aside thinking it had nothing to do with them.

JR: On the other hand, people did respond quickly in Ontario after the election of Mike Harris. There were demonstrations every single week, and some of the most massive demonstrations we have ever seen in Canada. Resistance to the cuts is important. But unless we can come up with clear alternatives, we are certain to lose the war, even if we manage to win a battle or two.

There are certain weaknesses I see on the Left, a certain small "c" conservatism which means that people are not very anxious to look at new ideas. There is a bunker mentality that comes from having to fight on so many different fronts. But there is also the problem that many groups have a vested interest in the status quo. Social service agencies are afraid to lose government funding, so they co-operate with workfare even though they abhor it in principle. Unions are seriously divided over strategy, with one wing wanting to move out in alliance with social movements to organize a massive fightback and the other clinging to the old method of "wait until the next election and elect the NDP." There is a backlash even on the Left to the transformative work that the women's movement has done in making our organizations truly representative and anti-racist.

During the free trade debate, many of us somehow wound up defending a status quo that we never supported. Women's groups have always been against big bureaucracies delivering services in health care and social assistance, but it is hard to come up with more democratic forms of service delivery when the Right is pushing for privatization. It's easy to say, "Stop the cuts." But that's just putting our fingers in a dike that is sprouting more and more holes.

KR: We know that the issues have gotten a lot more complex. It is very challenging to be talking about global economic restructuring, and it is difficult to mobilize people to fight abstract concepts like monetarism. Yet these questions impact on our lives directly. Our job as community organizers and activists is to simplify these issues so that we can identify what our priorities should be and then sharpen our demands. I shouldn't have to feel like I need a degree in economics to have a say in my future. Economics is really just about politics, values. It's about how we use our resources to get what we need and reflect what we believe. We need to pull it down to that level and get away from the intimidating rhetoric about debt and deficit that the Right want to hold us hostage to. There's such brainwashing going on now; it's even hitting little children. Recently a group of schoolchildren raised money to give to the prime minister to help pay the debt. I'm sure those kids don't even understand what debt and deficit are, but they've been told, "This is the monster that is eating away at your future." It's disturbing. As governments build more casinos and encourage people to gamble and to attack the poor, I'd like to see every sector of society, including faith communities, come out more strongly in voicing opposition. We have to reach out to everybody and have engaging debates, forums where people can educate each other and get involved.

Another problem that has happened with the Left is that many academics have gotten totally bogged down with postmodern theorizing and are removed from the real world. The need to challenge the political philosophies and practices of the Right is there, but it has gone unmet. A lot of academics have totally cut themselves off from progressive movements. But they are often the ones who are in the best position to assist movements in coming up with new strategies, because they have the resources to do it.

JR: Yes, we need more left-wing think tanks to develop alternatives. The Canadian Centre for Policy Alternatives is doing some excellent work, and the National Action Committee on the Status of Women is planning a feminist research body. We need to put forward a whole series of concrete alternatives on the political, economic and social level. But we also need an instrument to carry out the policy—a political party. We don't have any political parties, at least in the North, that are expressing an alternate vision in this stage of capitalism. Social democratic parties by and large are caving in to conservative economic policies. Because we live in an electoral democracy, an alternate vision has to be expressed through a political party or else it doesn't have the weight it needs to affect public policy. These days just talking in a positive way about the role of government in job creation and protection of social programs, as B.C. NDP leader Glen Clark has done, sounds positively revolutionary.

Feminism has done very well, so much so that it's very hard now to attack the idea that women should be equal. But somehow we haven't addressed social inequality well enough. It may be that the problem of youth unemployment in a sense will help us do that, because if you have a generation of young people who have no future, you can't survive as a society.

KR: Left-wing movements have to develop and encourage youth participation and leadership. We need to stop asking, "Where are the youth?" and start going to where they are and listening to what they have to say. Ironically, the people who are most concerned about what youth think and how they feel are advertisers, because they want to know how pitch their products.

JR: We're in a stronger position in the North because of the nature of the work force—it's better educated, has more resources, is more powerful and better organized to resist some of this. I was inspired by the demonstration in Hamilton, Ontario, of 120,000 people, in which you saw teachers, one of the most conservative groups in society, out there protesting against the cuts. That's an educated, privileged sector out on the streets with auto workers and steel workers and construction workers protesting this restructuring of society. That's very powerful. I think we have to talk in much clearer class terms now. When we talk about cuts to social programs, wages, working conditions, attacks on union rights, deregulation . . . all of these weaken the organized power of workers and other social groups and strengthen business and the elites. One of the big problems with postmodernism is that it ignores the reality of class divisions in society.

And for all the strength of the Right, they are appealing to the worst in people: selfishness, individualism and resentment. I'm enough of a democrat to believe that appeals to generosity and solidarity, as long as they are based on realistic possibilities for change, will be more successful.

2

A Distorting Lens

MAINSTREAM MEDIA

KR: The media has a lot of power. Most of what we know about what's going on in the world we find out through the media. I think the media's even greater power is its power to expose injustice. But as women, people of colour, poor people and social activists, we find that the media mostly ignores or distorts our reality rather than exposing the injustices we face. If we look at some of the reasons why and how this happens, then we get a better sense of the possibilities of changing it.

JR: A good recent example is the way the national media ignored the Women's March against Poverty sponsored by NAC and the Canadian Labour Congress in the spring of 1996. The march was an extraordinary event that took place over an entire month, with caravans visiting ninety communities and events involving about 50,000 women from coast to coast. Yet the national media did not cover the march at all until it arrived in Toronto, where it was greeted by a large demonstration. At the same time, when a small group of New Right old boys—and young boys—had a private meeting in Calgary called Winds of Change (or, as I prefer to call it, Windbags of Change), they got massive coverage. Their meeting was supposed to plot out a strategy to unify the Right, but it accomplished absolutely nothing. The women's march, on the other hand, culminated in a demonstration in Ottawa that turned out to be the largest women's protest in Canadian history.

The Windbags meeting got covered because it was seen as a grouping of powerful people and because it was something new. Of course the women's march was also something new, but over the last few years, the media has decided that NAC is not powerful or influential, and therefore they have ignored NAC's activities. One of the things that really drives me crazy is how the media will ignore what a group does and then denounce the group for being marginal.

KR: The women's march was also historically significant and powerful because it represented a joining of the labour movement and the women's movement in an unprecedented cross-Canada action, and this should have been newsworthy. But because the media has such a limited notion of what power is, they have traditionally sidelined social movements until those movements reach a point where it's impossible to ignore them.

JR: Power is one attraction for the media, but the other one is conflict, and there was no conflict on this march. There was both power and conflict in the Windbags story: the power of the Right and the conflict between the Tories and the Reform Party.

KR: A few years ago, I was at a conference for young women that was put on by the Canadian Advisory Council on the Status of

Women. A big network sent a reporter, and she stayed the full two or three days that the conference was going on. At the end, after hearing all of these young women talking and realizing on their own that feminism is a positive force, the reporter assembled me and a couple of other women. We came from different backgrounds, we were different ages, we had some differing ideas about what feminism actually meant, but we agreed that feminism is a good thing. The reporter wanted to put us on a morning TV talk show. She called up her producers, and we sat in the room and watched her battle over the phone to get this story of what the conference meant to us on the air. One of the producers interviewed each of us over the phone and then told the reporter that there was no story because none of us was saying that feminism is bad, and we weren't disagreeing with each other. There was no cat fight, so no story. The media have started a whole line about how no one wants to call herself a feminist any more. But then you have this diverse group of young women from across Canada embracing the term, and the story is dropped because it doesn't fit into the media's mould.

JR: This kind of thing happens all the time. You have to fit into their idea of the story or you don't get coverage. If a reporter is assigned to do a story on how NAC has become marginal because of its focus on racism, for example, she will find someone to quote who will say that. Even if the reporter talks to twenty women who think NAC has never been more relevant and only one who is prepared to make the criticism her editor wants, the story will read as if this one woman's opinion is a general criticism in the women's movement. It is a rare reporter who will challenge her editor on the framing of such a story.

I think it's instructive to look at media coverage of the women's movement in the eighties versus coverage in the nineties, because it has changed significantly. In the eighties women's groups and left-wing social action groups got a lot of coverage in Canada. That wasn't so true in other countries. But things changed in Canada after the defeat of the Charlottetown Accord in 1992. I just did a search of all *Globe and Mail* stories published between 1988 and 1995 that mention NAC. In 1988 there were 64 stories; in 1990, 72 articles; in 1992 (referendum year), 185. In 1994 it was down to 48, and in 1995 there were only 45. It is my impression that the coverage has diminished because when NAC played such a central role in Charlottetown as a major leader of the "No" campaign, we overstepped the bounds of what social action groups are permitted. We had too big an influence on the outcome. The whole attack on "special interest groups," which had been promoted for a long time by the federal Tories and the Reform Party, started to be taken up by the media. So now we have a situation where social action groups are almost entirely shut out of the media unless there is a big demonstration or something. For example, when the Council of Canadians held a press conference the day after the Quebec referendum to speak against decentralization, they got no media coverage. They had a whole platform of proposed change in response to the referendum—different powers for Quebec, the maintaining of a strong central government, an elected Senate with proportional representation. It was an absolutely opposite vision to the one the Reform Party is putting out. And here the *Globe and Mail* was, writing editorials about how we need another vision for Canada, yet giving zero coverage to the Council of Canadians, a very significant Canadian nationalist organization.

Another factor here is that the media sees politics as parliamentary politics. So since the last federal election, when the NDP was decimated, the media has decided that the Left no longer exists, and therefore that groups like NAC, the Canadian Labour

Congress and the Council of Canadians have no influence. But I
think things like the massive demonstrations in Ontario against
the Harris government, Glen Clark's re-election in B.C. and the
success of the Women's March against Poverty will start to turn
this around.

The media is supposed to reflect reality, but in fact it constructs
reality. Clearly the media has to select what it produces, but given
the lack of diversity in its ranks, the selection takes place in the
context of clear class, gender and racial bias. And because of the
pack mentality of the media, there can be whole periods, like the
last few years, or particular issues, like economics, where dissenting voices are almost totally silenced.

KR: The mainstream media is a corporate entity that takes corporate interests to heart. I know it's not a conspiracy, and no one
person makes sure that nothing radical gets into the news. But a
whole lot of different factors come together to shape the media's
biases. Reporters are only one part of it. You can find some sympathetic reporters. But they've got to answer to editors who have
to please publishers who have to produce competitive products
and meet the needs of the corporation.

Business interests were very evident in the way Conrad Black's
Hollinger Inc. took over three Saskatchewan dailies and laid off
nearly two hundred people. In the words of one executive, even
though the papers were making a profit, it wasn't a big enough
profit. The spin-off effect of the layoffs for these papers is a
smaller staff, which means less time and resources to do good
investigative journalism or local reporting.

JR: And now Black has bought a lot of Thomson papers and a
controlling interest in Southam, which means that one man will
own almost half of the daily newspapers in English Canada. This

is very scary, especially given Black's extremely right-wing views and his activism as a publisher. But the problem isn't only corporate concentration. Today, it is almost impossible for an independent daily newspaper to survive financially. So more and more newspapers are being bought by huge corporations. For me, whether it is three corporations or ten corporations who own them is not that significant, since all the corporations have similar interests.

KR: I don't agree. I think corporate concentration *is* an important issue. It's ironic that the same people who harp on and on about how large public institutions like Canada Post are not competitive say absolutely nothing when a tremendous amount of media power is concentrated into the hands of a single individual. It's true that all newspaper owners might have similar class interests, but the greater the number of owners, the better our chances are for getting a diversity of opinion.

But increased corporate power in general can have a huge impact on the way world affairs are covered. The Persian Gulf War in 1991 illustrates that very well. The Gulf War turned into a showcase for the defence industry's missiles and other high-tech war equipment. We learned more about what kind of missiles were being dropped on the people of Iraq than we learned about why the war was happening. We learned that the U.S. soldiers stationed in the Gulf were drinking Pepsi.

JR: So one big component of the media coverage there was that major military companies were advertising their weapons. But if you said that to a journalist covering the war, that person would be outraged, because that is not what was in their head when they were reporting.

KR: Yeah, but where did the reporters get their information about what was actually happening? From the Pentagon, the U.S. army. That was their only source. The army had a sophisticated media strategy to get their message out, and they prevented reporters from going certain places. Images of thousands of innocent citizens being injured or killed would not have made this a "popular" war. Ramsey Clark, the former U.S. attorney general, travelled to Iraq shortly after the war was over and got video footage of the devastating impact of those missiles. No network would show them. Yet the myth of a free, unbiased press continues.

JR: Using the media for propaganda purposes during a war is nothing new, but I noticed the same kind of media tunnel vision during the NGO conference held in conjunction with the United Nations women's conference in China in 1995. All the western media reported on the same thing. They reported on the Chinese government's attempts to place restrictions on the conference, and on the harassment of delegates and the poor physical conditions of the site, rather than reporting on the content of the NGO conference itself. Why? The initial story got good play, for one thing. It was certainly a legitimate news story when the Chinese unilaterally changed the NGO conference site from Beijing to Huairou and were refusing visas to some delegates. But once the conference got going, the Chinese authorities did everything possible to facilitate it. Yet the media continued to find every problem they could to back up their contention that the Chinese were trying to sabotage the conference. The original story played into the desire of the western power elite to show the Chinese government in a bad light, and the media continued to take that angle. The other news story, of course, was whatever the delegates did at the official UN conference in Beijing, because what political leaders do and say is always news. So the content of the official conference got covered, but the content of the NGO conference didn't.

The western media has been predicting the death of feminism off and on for about fifteen years now. Yet here was a conference of 35,000 to 45,000 women from every country in the world. That was almost twice as many as had attended the conference held in Nairobi ten years before, but hardly anyone considered that news. The plenary sessions at the conference focussed on globalization and on the cuts being made everywhere to social spending at the same time as military spending is increasing. Woman after woman made strong links between the struggles in the South against structural adjustment and the struggles for equality in the North, but no one considered that news. The conference documented the enormous strides made by women in the South in the last ten years, where the women's movement has been organizing in almost every country, but that too was not news. Even the shocking exposure of the sex trade in Asia was not news.

There was certainly a strong dose of sexism in the media's failure to report on the content of the conference, too. As one of the speakers said, "What we have here is the largest group of marginalized experts in the world."

KR: When you look at the media's portrayal of African-Canadian communities, you can see that the media is not just ignoring us, it's distorting our reality. When you see Black faces, usually male, they are in crime stories or on the sports pages. This limited coverage alienates us and cements negative images in the minds of white people who have no connection with people of diverse communities. It ends up perpetuating prejudices. I don't think people are mindless sponges who believe everything they hear or read. But there's very little counterbalancing the negativity. And while images of Blacks are distorted, images of Asians, South Asians and Latinos are practically nonexistent in the mainstream media. That's why I find it so laughable when right-wingers carry on about "multiculturalism gone too far." Listen to CBC Radio, watch TV, drop into the newsrooms of any major daily in Canada. Where are the people of colour? CNDA, the Canadian Daily Newspaper Association, did a survey of forty-one different news-rooms in 1994 and found that less than 3 per cent of journalists were people of colour, at least five times less than the percentage we make up of the general population.

JR: Representation is important, but it doesn't solve the prob-lem. Women are well represented now in the media. The Canadian feminist organization Media Watch did an international survey in which they found that women made up almost 50 per cent of journalists internationally but only 15 per cent of sources cited. Most women journalists are still conforming to the male definition of news, power and conflict, and they are often afraid to challenge their editors and producers about what and who is news. On the other hand, being *does* determine consciousness, and if we ever had any question about that, we can just look at the record of the "Globe and Male."

The all-male editorial board of the *Globe and Mail* wrote four editorials attacking the University of British Columbia's chilly cli-mate report and the subsequent actions of the university admin-istration to attempt to deal with charges of sexual and racial harassment in the political science department there. I agree there were problems with the report, but the *Globe* waged a holy war against it. In addition to the editorials, there were six columns, fourteen news stories, two features and countless letters to the editor. Only the letters to the editor expressed any alternate opinion to the other coverage. At about the same time, at the

University of Manitoba, two women hired as professors in the all-male political science department were sexually harassed so badly that they both quit their jobs. The *Globe* virtually ignored the University of Manitoba story, making only a small mention of it in a feature about sexual harassment. No one at U.B.C. lost their job as a result of the chilly climate report; no one was even disciplined. But at the University of Manitoba two young female professors were driven out of the department and the university, and this was not considered newsworthy.

Coverage of the issues around the Writing thru Race conference in Vancouver in 1994 is another example. Writers of colour in a mainstream organization, the Writers' Union of Canada, wanted to meet to talk to each other. Big deal. Women's groups have been doing that for decades. But the furor in the media was incredible. The thing that infuriated me most was that it was the media who savaged that conference. It began with a column by Robert Fulford in the *Globe and Mail.* When the Reform Party picked it up, government funding was withdrawn. The Writers' Union held the conference anyway, because a lot of people supported it financially. And then, of course, there were very few media reports about the conference itself.

KR: For Blacks, there is a particular mistrust of the media because of the differential treatment we get. Just look at the editorial and opinion columns of a paper like the *Toronto Sun.* Freedom-of-the-press arguments cannot justify comments from columnists like McKenzie Porter, whose writings championed apartheid in South Africa. We've seen the protests and heard the grievances of white fishers about the lack of work in Atlantic Canada, but the Black community in Halifax has successfully organized a sit-in that at this point has gone on for more than two months, at a Canada Employment Centre serving the African-

Canadian community that the federal government wants to shut down. Here you have a story of a community dramatically pulling together for a round-the-clock protest against high unemployment, and it gets no national press. But when the fights between white and Black kids broke out at Cole Harbour, we all heard about it.

Or take the Arnold Minors story. Arnold Minors, who sat on the police services board in Toronto, said to a reporter that the police were perceived by some in the Black community to be an occupying army. Well, his comment was distorted, and instead he was portrayed as saying that *he* thinks the police are an occupying force. The story dragged on for weeks and actually led to an investigation of Minors by a provincial government body. Meanwhile, the police chief at the time, William McCormack, made a similar comment, saying that some see the police as an occupying army. Nothing happened to McCormack as a result.

JR: I think there are two elements to what you are talking about. One is racism pure and simple. The racism that, because he is Black and on the police board, the media are looking for Arnold Minors to be biased. They accept and even expect a pro-police bias on the part of most members of the police commission, but they are looking for a Black person on the police board to be biased in favour of the Black community and against the police. There's another kind of racism at work here, too, that has to do with the fact things look different from the point of view of the Black community than they do from the point of view of the white community. Since the media are almost all white, they see things from that point of view.

KR: The big media outlets know quite well that their staff is not diverse, but it's just not on their agenda to change. CDNA did a poll of publishers in 1993 where they were asked to rank their level of concern about issues facing newspapers. Out of twenty-one issues, diversity was nineteenth. Despite that, it's important to remember that groups like the Urban Alliance on Race Relations have worked to make positive changes, and things are better today, even though we have a long way to go.

JR: Another aspect of all this is that anybody who fights against the status quo is going to be targeted. I was stereotyped in the media when I was president of NAC. Sure, I was angry in some speeches, but those were always the clips they used of me. So I came across as a humourless, angry, bitter person, which is exactly the opposite of who I am. There is an element of sexism in this as well, of course. After all, we all know that feminists are angry, ball-busting bitches. I didn't really notice the extent of the stereotyping until we started getting letters to *Face Off* about how surprised our viewers were that I was nice and had a sense of humour.

So when you add it all up, whole portions of the community feel as if their lives aren't reflected in the media at all. The question is, what do we do about it? We live in a media-driven society, and social activists need to see the media as a site of activism. I get frustrated, because when people disagree with something government does they have no problem organizing against it, but when they disagree with the media, they are totally passive about it.

KR: We have to hold the media accountable, but we can't keep playing the blame game. It doesn't get us anywhere and it makes us feel powerless. The media is not in the business of doing public relations for social movements, and we have to realize that, without serious concerted demands for change in the media, they won't respond.

JR: I don't think "demands" is the right way to think about it. I think "challenges" is a better way. For example, before the NAC annual general meeting in 1996, outgoing president Sunera Thobani strongly criticized the lack of media coverage of the Women's March against Poverty on *Face Off* and debated the point with my co-host, Claire Hoy, at some length. She obviously struck a chord, because within a couple of days both *Morningside* and *As It Happens* had discussions about this. I think Sunera's challenge resulted in increased media coverage of the final days of the march and of the NAC AGM.

KR: But you can only challenge the media if you have some access to it already. If you are completely outside of it, and are consistently portrayed in a negative light, then you have to make demands. So, for example, I think that the Black community needs to demand that more journalists of colour be hired, and that progressive people need to demand column space and a greater presence in radio and TV spots.

JR: There is no question about it. I think my presence on *Face Off* every night has had an important influence on others in the media, especially at the CBC. But people are very passive about supporting journalists who reflect alternate views. When Doris Anderson, a strong feminist and a good writer, was replaced as a columnist in the *Toronto Star* by Donna LaFramboise, who does little but attack the women's movement, there was very little protest. On the other hand, when the *Globe* ran that disgusting "Men" column—which at one point applauded a U.S. magazine that warned of more violence against women if feminists didn't stop whining—people did protest, including *Globe* journalists, and eventually the column was dropped. I think journalists themselves and their organizations have to take more responsibility to ensure that a diversity of opinion and experience is reflected in the media.

In terms of influencing coverage, one way to do that is to meet with editorial boards and point out their bias. Sometimes this works, and sometimes it doesn't. Usually it works only in areas where the publisher or editor doesn't have a vested interest and the errors are more of omission than commission, though. When I was part of an Action Canada Network meeting with various editorial boards on how the media were not covering opposition to NAFTA, we didn't get very far.

Another way to influence coverage is through media monitoring. The right-wing Fraser Institute has a media watch. They publish their criticism of what they believe is a liberal bias in the media, and it has an impact. The feminist organization Media Watch does an excellent job of monitoring the media for the representation of women and minorities and for female stereotyping, but I think what we need in Canada is an organization, like FAIR (Fairness and Accuracy in Reporting) in the United States, that is going to do wide-ranging monitoring of the media and publicize the results. A recent *Globe and Mail* article on Canadian think tanks revealed that the Fraser Institute was cited 139 times in the *Globe*, and the left-wing Centre for Policy Alternatives was cited 18 times. The article saw this as a sign of how effective think tanks are, but I think we could argue that what it really reflects is the *Globe*'s bias. That is the kind of thing we need to do. We need to document the bias of the media, because they don't believe they are biased.

KR: The myth of objectivity. I think it's that same myth that demands there be supposed "equal time" in media coverage. Like on your show, *Face Off*, you present the Left view and the Right view. But the Right view has the advantage of being spread by the government, other major media, business and Hollywood, so it's not really "balanced."

If we want better, more diverse news coverage on a consistent basis, we're not going to get it by making individual comments or complaints here and there. We're going to have to work for change on a long-term basis. We're going to have to raise concerns about the concentration of ownership into the hands of a few and fight against the privatization of our public systems.

JR: Yes. The CBC, for example, is dying of a thousand cuts, and there is not enough public protest. What I find is that people get angry that the CBC doesn't represent diversity well enough, so they don't feel compelled to defend against cuts and privatization. But what we should be doing is pressuring the CBC to represent Canada better, like FAIR does with PBS in the United States. At the same time, we have to defend the CBC from cutbacks, because it is a precious resource for the people of Canada.

KR: We need to have our own ways of communicating our strategies and ideas, too, to one another and to as large an audience as possible. Alternate media has been one way of doing this. In the Black communities across the country there are dozens of community newspapers. That is where people go to find out what is really going on. We are able to exchange information and political ideas. And sometimes stories even get picked up and reprinted in the mainstream media. But we are still seeing exclusion happening at a lot of levels, especially in radio and on television.

Black communities have made two attempts to get the CRTC to approve an all-Black radio station, and both times they were turned down. It was claimed that there wasn't enough need for this kind of a station, even though we know that there are all kinds of different radio stations that play Black music all the time. There are a lot of people in our community who are very experienced in radio work. Yet our application was turned down and place on the dial was given to yet another country and western station. The only place you can hear Black voices regularly on radio is on small community radio stations. When we are on bigger stations, you have to listen to the graveyard shift, because that is the only time slot given to talk shows on community issues. An all-Black community radio station would be great, and not just for us; anybody could tune in and listen to these voices that they don't usually hear.

JR: I think the space for alternate voices in general is narrowing. The feminist press has really declined. The only regularly published paper we have is *Kinesis. Herizons,* a feminist magazine, comes out irregularly. And the Left press in Canada is also very weak. We have *THIS Magazine, Canadian Dimension* and *Canadian Forum,* but their circulation and profile are low. Probably the most successful alternate media is radio. Co-op Radio in Vancouver is a real institution, and in other cities university radio stations provide an alternate source of information and music. In the United States, on the other hand, there is a huge alternate media. And even American mainstream magazines like *Harper's* and *The New Yorker* have some interesting debates about real issues.

I think lack of resources is a big part of the problem. I also think that because the Left in Canada has had more access to the mainstream media, there has been less of a priority placed on establishing alternate media here. This is of course less true for minority communities. A couple of years ago a group of people in Toronto and Vancouver were seriously discussing the possibility of putting out a national alternative newspaper with a left-wing editorial slant. They had a fairly large financial contribution to get started. Their plan was to launch something quite professional and attract left-wing journalists who are looking for a broader outlet for their ideas. There was a lot of interest, but in the end they decided they didn't have enough money to get it off the ground.

Alternatives are important, but they're not a substitute for better coverage in the mainstream media.

KR: For all its problems, the mainstream media does have the power to expose injustice, and social movements have been able to use the media effectively. If we think about it from a historical perspective, we have been doing this for a long time. The civil rights movement had the impact it did because of national and international coverage. People around the world could see Black people demonstrating in the streets and police turning dogs on them, the actual brutality of the racist, white supremacist state. And this has been true more recently with South Africa and apartheid. I don't want to beat up on the mainstream media entirely, because in some cases it does expose wrongs.

We on the Left have to be more aware of the news media's demands. Reporters need to meet strict deadlines, and they want us to give them visuals and to summarize our ideas in sound bites. They gravitate to events and individuals, not issues. And we're competing for attention against political parties and think tanks with public relations staff. Getting good at this game takes a lot of practice.

But often what the media want in terms of a story can compromise the message we want to get out. Recently I was talking to a long-time reporter who was telling me that journalists are tired of covering standard press conferences; they want human interest stories. Fair enough. But sometimes when they focus on specific individuals, we lose the big picture.

JR: I don't think we can overcome the bias of the media, but we can learn how to use the media as effectively as possible, how to use openings. A good example of that is what NAC did with the refugee women campaign. In the fall of 1992, there was a lot of news about the mass rapes in Bosnia, and in Canada there was the case of Nada, a Saudi Arabian woman claiming refugee status because back home she would be persecuted for refusing to wear the veil. The NAC executive decided this might be a good time to move forward with the issue of gender persecution as a basis for refugee status. We had a press conference where I declared that Canada should open its doors to abused women. At first there was negative reaction, but in fact we had hit a nerve. We followed up by making public the cases of fourteen women who were seeking refugee status on the basis of various forms of gender persecution, mostly domestic violence. Within months, the refugee board had changed its policy. Canada broke new ground, and now the principle has been picked up at the international level. We accomplished that almost exclusively through a media campaign based on work that had been going on at a grassroots level. We just picked the right time to raise it up to a public level.

KR: Even when you get bad coverage it can work to your advantage, because your supporters can read between the lines. I was involved in a campaign in Toronto against an anti-African art exhibit. A feature in the *Toronto Star* dismissed our protest as a "curious show." It accused us of being conspiracy theorists and said our position was "bizarre" and "extreme." But activists in the States saw the story, contacted our group and gave us invaluable information that we used to lobby the art gallery's board. And the gallery in Philadelphia, where the show was to travel next, considerably changed the exhibit because they feared the same controversy would happen there. The Black community protested the

Royal Ontario Museum's "Into the Heart of Africa" exhibit because it glorified imperialism. That became a big story. Media coverage wasn't always sympathetic. But I think it contributed to the decision of museums in Vancouver, Los Angeles and Albuquerque to back out of the scheduled tour of this exhibit.

We definitely need to keep strategizing around how to get what we want from the media, because nothing else reaches millions of people the way it does. The media impacts on our ability to think about issues, our ability to think about solving problems and about how we relate to the rest of the world.

JR: And we shouldn't accept that just because the media is mostly in private hands it's okay for them to do whatever the hell they want. Media is a central feature of democracy, and it has to be more accountable and representative.

3

Jobs, Jobs, No Jobs

THE FUTURE OF WORK

KR: The way the economy is heading means more and more people are getting caught in a low-pay—or no-pay—situation. I'm lucky in that I've been able to work with my family and do other things on the side. But when I think of the people I know who are my age and slightly older, many are unemployed, laid off, working on short-term contract, working part-time. Most of the new jobs being created are minimum-wage jobs and contract jobs with no benefits, and most are in the service sector, where we find a lot of women and young people today. Seventy per cent of part-time workers are women, with a lot of them wanting full-time work and not being able to find it. And there are also a lot of women working in isolation, doing piecework and home work. But what's really incredible about all this is that we're living in a time where banks and corporations are making huge profits and productivity is high, yet people's wages have not kept pace and people have less time to spend with their families or upgrade their education. So there is something askew in the whole system. We're creating all this wealth but not enjoying the benefits of it. Technology has helped create wealth but it has also brought less of a need for human labour in manufacturing and so on. The other thing is that, the way our economy is set up, there are always a certain number of people who remain unemployed and who need welfare. I think that poses a lot of questions for progressive people about how we move towards redistributing wealth instead of just demanding more jobs. The jobs we are getting are not secure, and we're also seeing governments making it harder for workers to organize and to have a safe and healthy workplace.

JR: Over the last few years, profitable companies in the private sector have been laying off employees. Now we're seeing the same kind of thing in the public sector, where the Right is arguing that we have to have smaller government. You hear people say, "Well, too bad for the public sector workers. We don't have job security in the private sector, so why should they?" Divide and conquer. The Left is correct to a point: defend the jobs, and if you can't defend the jobs, at least defend the rights of the workers being laid off to have the best possible security in that layoff, including job readjustment programs. The idea argued by many mainstream economists that the economy functions best at 8 or 9 per cent unemployment is unacceptable.

But there is an opportunity in this crisis to talk about different ways of organizing work than the one we're accustomed to. Feminists have long pointed out that unpaid work is undervalued and that economic emphasis has been only on work outside the home. I don't think that's going to change, but I do think that sharing the work and sharing the wealth is the right way to look at it. So we should be arguing for things like a ban on overtime to start with, a shorter work week, longer parental leave, family leave, and more emphasis placed on men taking responsibility at home and taking care of children. These things need to get integrated into a whole different approach to jobs and family and community, where there's more value placed on home and community life and less value on what you do in the workplace.

KR: One way this change could begin to happen would be if men, who dominate the area of paid and publicly recognized work, were to do more community and domestic work. That would open up opportunities for women and young people. The frustration women are feeling is not just with a double work day but with a huge amount of insecurity, because it's hard to make long-term plans on a short-term income. And on top of that, they're having to pay someone else to look after their children. Youth are feeling very demoralized; they're probably better educated than any previous generation, but there's no place to develop their talents and skills. So middle-class twenty-somethings do some work/study abroad thing, like moving to Asia to teach English, or they stay in school and rack up a bigger student-loan debt to do another degree. And then there's the whole moving-back-in-with-your-parents trend. Meanwhile, poorer youth are scrambling to just get by on shrinking welfare benefits. The government's response, putting bursts of cash into short-term projects, doesn't do much to deal with all of this insecurity. A whole new generation is not getting the training or the skills we need in order to manage our society or to plan what it is going to look like in the next twenty, forty or fifty years.

JR: I think we're seeing a few people at the top, and that will include some select young people, who are going to be doing better and better, increasing their wealth, like these CEOs whose salaries are enormous at the same time as they are cutting workers right, left and centre. Some will do very well, but most won't have a chance. That polarization is happening among women, too. Even though some are doing a lot better, most women are starting to do a lot worse. So I think it's not so much that we're not training people for leadership in the future as it is that the share of wealth, the share of a decent life, is narrowing and will narrow further and further as we go on. The question becomes, how do we change that? I think part of the answer is to look at this issue of work time vs. family life.

KR: I'm just saying that comparatively more people of my generation are not getting any kind of work at all. But instead of people understanding the frustrations we face, we're called slackers, the "lost generation." What's *lost* are the good jobs, the opportunities. We can't all be entrepreneurs, computer programmers or casino workers. Very often discussions about work try to pit older workers against younger workers and vice versa, and that's destructive. But it comes from insecurity. If young people are absent from the union movement, it's mostly because they are unemployed or working in jobs where there are no unions. That's a problem that must be addressed. It'd be good if we could teach youth how to organize, how unions work, whether they're in the work force right now or not.

JR: I agree. My generation didn't face a lack of jobs. Youth unemployment today is verging on a crisis. The rates are phenomenal, twice and three times the unemployment levels for older people. Government is responding with band-aid youth training and employment programs, but they should also be playing a role in creating jobs. A national child-care program is a good example of a place where we could create new jobs that are socially useful and satisfying and could hopefully pay a decent wage.

KR: In parts of Africa and the Caribbean, the way women are surviving is by creating small businesses for themselves, sometimes along with doing other work. In Canada, some women have set up community economic development projects. For example, in North Bay a group of twelve Somali women, recent immigrants, were in a course together learning English, and they decided to work with each other. They got help to identify their strengths and develop a business plan. With a little seed money, they formed a small clothing manufacturing co-op, and they ended up selling all the clothes they made in 1995. It was a good start, but to keep it going they would need more start-up cash, which is hard to get from banks. So there are limits, but the women made some money and they were in control of the whole project, and that was satisfying. Community economic development is one alternative, but I think we have to figure out how to reorganize the whole economy to benefit the majority.

JR: In the sixties we thought technology would bring us more leisure time, but instead it has created greater profits, greater return on investment for a few people. Everyone should be able to benefit from technological change, not just the select few. We have to think of concrete ways to make that a reality. Right now we have the abstract notion of the value of unpaid labour, the private/public sphere stuff, demands around job creation and labour readjustment, and transitional demands like a shorter work week, or a guaranteed annual income. We have to find a way to move those demands forward in a realistic way.

KR: But what makes it difficult is that the changes are happening so fast, and people are just struggling to hold on to what they have. In the Maritimes, for example, the fishing industry has dried up and people are at their wits' end So it seems there's no room or place for them to sit down and think about how to restructure the economy. There's no one grand solution to rectify all situations. I think unions, academics and economists can play a huge role in terms of developing some alternatives. But we're in such a crunch with governments rolling back progressive workplace laws now that unions have placed a lot of their attention on just trying to meet some basic demands. It's hard to defend what you have, or fight for what you had, and put forth a whole new solution at the same time.

JR: I think unions have always played a major role in developing alternatives, and some of them are still able to do that. Things like pay equity, employment equity and even child care were bargained collectively before we thought of organizing to get legislation. One current example is the Canadian Auto Workers, who last year bargained a ban on mandatory overtime. That is a huge accomplishment for a union, because its own members want the money that comes from working overtime, but it was their way of sharing jobs. By banning mandatory overtime, they're creating more jobs. Of course it's in the interest of the employers to have overtime, because then they don't have all the costs of hiring new people. It was a struggle inside the union to convince people that it was in their best interests to share the work. Unions used to be completely against job-sharing. I remember when they saw it as a way to break unions, break seniority. Now they are much more flexible about it.

Another area I think the unions have to examine is their

pension funds. There are billions of dollars in union pension funds that are now being administered by employers. By legislation, these funds have to be invested to produce maximum returns. What that means is that union members' money is part of the large pool of investment capital that is pressuring companies to make maximum profits. I think this pool of capital could be a huge source of power for working people. And I believe if we could create real alternatives for investment of that money that would help create jobs and protect social services, union members would agree to change the direction of their pension funds.

Where we haven't really succeeded in raising work/time issues is on the political level. That's because at the moment right-wing economic ideas control the agenda, and the Right's line is that in order to be more competitive, we have to downsize and workers have to be more flexible, meaning prepared to lose their jobs any time. The Right argues this as if the interests of employers and workers were one. But of course we've got conflicting interests here. It's also hard to put forward these work/time issues now because wages are not increasing, so people need as much work as they can get. If they're in a position where they can get more work and make more money they'll do it, because they want that for their families. So it's really a tough issue to struggle through. The fact that some unions have taken it on is to their credit.

KR: I think people forget that the union movement has made so many changes that the entire society has benefited from. Our health care system, standard holidays and break time, unemployment insurance and all kinds of social programs came about as a result of workers' struggles. But today the challenge lies in expanding and revitalizing union membership and leadership. Only about one-third of Canadian workers are unionized, and it's very tough for unions to organize in some areas, the private service sector, for example. Women coming to Canada from different parts of the world have realized this for a long time. Women from the Caribbean and the Philippines who do domestic work or work in hospitals or take care of the aged have really strenuous workloads and are often isolated from the rest of the community, so there's no opportunity for them to think about how to organize. The thing is that a lot of other people benefit from the work done by these women. People put their parents in old-age homes, rely on huge hospitals and in some cases rely on domestic workers to care for their children. So we still have to put a class picture in there as we talk about what's happening to these women. The whole society depends on their long workdays and low wages. The future of the labour movement depends on its ability to organize in these sectors. When contracting-out happens, often the new unorganized people brought in are immigrants and people of colour. The federal government used to employ the people who cleaned the postal service buildings, and so those workers belonged to the Public Service Alliance. But then, in the late eighties, they started contracting out the work to private companies who brought in low-paid cleaners with no union. There's definitely still a caste system in terms of who gets to do what kinds of work, who gets union support and representation and who doesn't. The Canadian Union of Postal Workers tried to organize these workers, but it's a struggle because the laws are used to protect private contractors.

JR: The problem with the service sector is that people's workplaces are small, meaning that if they do get a union, they don't have the power to negotiate. So then you have to look at cross-sectoral bargaining, where the whole sector in a particular region bargains together rather than having workplace by workplace bargaining. One of the good things about the Ontario labour bill brought in by the NDP under Bob Rae, but then overturned by the Tories, was that it included some elements that made it easier to organize in the service sector and really marginal sectors of the work force, like among cleaners. Of course the Right never talked about those aspects of the bill. They focussed on the measures in the bill that outlawed the use of scabs and suggested that the bill gave more power to "big labour," which is becoming the new scapegoat for everything.

The other point you raise has to do with diversity and anti-racism. So much of the work force in the urban centres is made up of people of colour. Just as there has been a struggle around sexism and affirmative action for women in the labour movement, the struggle to have more representation of people of colour has begun over the last couple of years. It isn't reflected in the leadership of the labour movement yet.

KR: If you look at the history, you see that workers of colour in Canada organized on their own, like the Black porters on the railway who were segregated into the lowest-paying jobs. Whites officially barred them from joining their unions. Unions have made a lot of progress. But more affirmative action has to happen inside the unions, especially in the leadership. I was talking to a friend who said she made a simple suggestion that the union she was working for hire some more Chinese people to teach Chinese workers English, and she was told that that would be "reverse discrimination." The stakes are really high today, because the place where women and people of colour have been able to get the best jobs, with the most security, decent wages and good benefits, is the public sector, which is now being decimated. This is especially true when we look at the question of union seniority provisions. Seniority rights are a hot potato right now, but we have to recognize too that for people of colour, who by and large have less

seniority, the classic scenario of "last hired, first fired" is still relevant. In Ontario, it was only in recent years that greater numbers
of people of colour got work in the public sector. Federally, there
was an increase in the number of women hired over the last five
or ten years, but this was not so true for people of colour.

JR: Our original idea of employment equity was quotas; basically, employers had to hire such and such a percentage of women,
such and such a percentage of minorities and so forth, but that
never really flew. It's ironic that every attack on employment
equity legislation has made a big deal about quotas, because no
legislation has ever contained a proposal for them.

There's always been a certain resistance to employment equity,
but the real backlash started with the economic recession, when
people began to worry about their own jobs. Things really started
to change in the nineties with economic uncertainty and the rise
of the Right. Of course, right-wing groups said employment
equity would mean that young white men wouldn't get jobs, that
what was happening was reverse discrimination.

Now it's a bit of a moot point because of cutbacks. The cutbacks have meant that in the areas where there is the most
commitment to employment equity, such as universities and government, nobody's hiring, and in addition there are layoffs that hit
the target groups harder.

KR: People have to realize that diversity is a strength. And if
restructuring is happening, personnel management should keep
that in mind. With firefighters, for example, some people still
believe you need a big burly guy to fight off a fire. But I heard a
woman firefighter talk about how her smaller build allowed her to
slip through openings in burning buildings that her larger male
colleagues couldn't fit through.

JR: Oh yes, firefighters are a hot one. But if you look at the federal statistics, employment equity has had very little impact on changing the composition of the workplace. In fact, equity doesn't exist in most places. So why all this anger? I think it's partly due to the fact that equality-seeking groups, through their own advocacy, have gotten a lot of public attention in the last twenty years. Then you have these young white men, whom nobody's paying attention to. When I taught university a few years back, one of the things that male students in my class used to say to me was, "Why should I have to pay the price for what my father did by being passed over for a job?" It's a fair question.

KR: Casting themselves in the role of victim is a very effective strategy, because it draws attention away from the entire history of discrimination and violation of human rights. Again and again we get the line, "Oh, why should I have to pay for slavery? Slavery was hundreds of years ago." But no amends have been made, so we're not on an equal footing. It's like somebody steals your pen and wants you to forgive him for it but doesn't want to give you the pen back first. It's a question of taking responsibility. White men today are definitely profiting from stolen lands, profiting from hundreds of years of affirmative action for *them*.

JR: I agree with you theoretically, but suppose I'm an eighteen-year-old white male high-school graduate. My father worked in an auto plant and was making thirty dollars an hour with a high-school diploma, right. I can't get that kind of job any more. All I can get is a job at McDonald's making minimum wage. So how did I profit, you see? I think that's a legitimate question.

I have a rule about the backlash. I think you have to stand up to the backlash, you can't back down, but on the other hand you have to look at why is there so much resonance for the backlash on the issue of employment equity. The reason is that there are fewer opportunities. That's true. But there are fewer opportunities because some people are getting very, very rich off of restructuring. So the strategy, it seems to me, for the women's movement or the anti-racist movement, is not to dismiss those people who oppose employment equity but to persuade them that it is fair.

KR: I'm just feeling this pit of frustration, because it puts people of colour and women once again into the unique position where, even as we struggle for our basic human rights, we have to take into account the anxiety and the anger of the people who are oppressing us. Oppressors never think about the victims' feelings, and never think about the hurt and the injustice and everything else that is still being done to people, and it's just tremendous, the wrongs that have happened. I'm forced to listen to what the powerful have to say every single day. They never see my reality reflected. There's a huge part of me that wants to say, just shut up, please.

JR: And maybe that part's right.

KR: It is right, but I still have to be practical. I have to learn to use that anger constructively. I have to get those people who are concerned about lost opportunities for white men to look around and ask, who is at the top? Who brought in the Free Trade Agreement and NAFTA, which made thousands of manufacturing jobs disappear? Who is privatizing everything and using technology against workers? Who is making profits but putting people out of work? And then who is driving taxi, cleaning hospital bedpans and doing the jobs Canadian-born people don't want to do anyway? You know, in 1985 the government did a study called *Who Gets the Work?*. They found that, on average, it is three times harder for a person of colour to get a job than a white person. Employment equity is about creating more fairness in society as a whole.

JR: And most people will agree that a workplace which includes women is an improvement over an all-male workplace, and a multicultural one an improvement over a monocultural one, but somehow employment equity still smacks to them of unfairness.

KR: The Right has been effective in convincing people that employment equity would undermine the merit principle. There are even a few people of colour who argue against affirmative action and employment equity, saying they don't want people to think they got a job because of an equity program. The thing is, you won't get a job because of a program, you'll get the job if you're qualified to do it. If you're not qualified, you won't be hired. What the program will do is help to ensure that if you *are* qualified, you won't get passed over because of your race, gender or disability. That's not a handout, it's a fair break. I think some people of colour are genuinely concerned about being stigmatized, and others criticize employment equity because they want to find favour with whites by saying, "I'm not gonna be one of those rabble-rousers." The first group of people should realize that, program or no program, if racism is there, it's there. Contrary to the reverse discrimination myth, measures to *combat* racism do not *create* racism. And there is nothing shameful about wanting to work and have a good job. The second group of people should realize that they and their children have benefited and will continue to benefit from all the struggles rabble-rousers win.

JR: The ferocity of the backlash explains it somewhat, but I still don't understand why, after fifteen years of fighting for it, we don't have more support among women and communities of people of colour for employment equity. When the Harris government announced they were going to get rid of Bill 79, the NDP employment equity bill, there was very little response. It appeared that nobody cared.

KR: I think there are several reasons why there wasn't a big outcry. First, even with all the coalition work, I don't think there were ever really a huge number of employment equity activists in Ontario, although there is broad general support for the idea in the target group communities. Second, it is always harder to mobilize people around long-term programmatic solutions, the effects of which they may not feel directly for a year, two years or more. It's been challenging and time-consuming to even explain how employment equity works and what we hoped it would do. And finally, I don't think people felt there was much they could do in the face of the Harris government's move. The writing was on the wall, and people are demoralized. The economy is bad, cutbacks are happening, small businesses are going bankrupt. I think the people who are most disadvantaged right now didn't believe employment equity would help them. To have gotten the government to back down on killing Bill 79 would have required a level of political fightback and organization that just wasn't possible to muster.

JR: I think the way to go now is to concentrate more of our energies on employers. When the affirmative action struggle started, it did not demand anything from the state: it demanded it from employers. It went after the company for discriminating. It was very successful, and not only with the employers who were targeted, like Stelco. In the late seventies, I got a job with McDonnell Douglas, an aircraft manufacturer. They decided they would hire a hundred women and see how it worked out. Of course, in the end hiring women was actually beneficial. And a lot of the bigger employers now are seeing that employment equity makes economic sense for them. One example is women on television. One of the reasons you see all these female anchors now is that women will watch a station that has a female anchor. That is strict bottom-line business. So there is the consumer power there.

I've always argued that we should target employers. At a certain point there was a particular grocery chain in Toronto that had all white cashiers. I said, "Why don't we go down and set up an information picket at that supermarket? We can say, 'They don't hire any people of colour. You should shop across the street, where there are people of colour.'" Very simple, right? But in the eighties we stopped doing all that and focussed everything on the state and on getting legislation.

KR: Activism got professionalized in a way. We became lobbyists. When you are spending so much energy on lobbying, then education and ties to the community disappear.

JR: Right. Because if you are lobbying for an employment equity bill and discussing whether the tribunal should have a pro-active or complaint-based model, there are about five people who know what you are talking about. Whereas if you are out in front of a supermarket handing out flyers, anybody can get involved. It's concrete and it's real.

And if there is a theme to these conversations you and I are having, this is it: we can't afford to just stick our fingers in the dike. We have to create new strategies for the new economic, political and social situation that we're facing.

I'd like us to move on from employment equity to talk a bit about the issue of guaranteed annual income. Not many people on

the Left support it any more. The union movement doesn't want
to give up unemployment insurance, and the poor people's groups
don't want to give up the welfare system the way it is now,
because they think they'll end up getting something worse. But I
think we have to consider both a guaranteed annual income and a
shorter work week as positive ways of dealing with the economic
changes we face. Both are important from the perspective of sharing wealth and making sure all of us benefit from technological
change, and also from a feminist perspective, since one of the
goals would be for men and women to share more of the values of
community and to spend more time with their families. I think a
guaranteed annual income at a living wage is important so that
people are not feeling so insecure about job instability. The only
way to achieve this kind of guaranteed income would be to collapse the U.I. and welfare programs and get rid of the bureaucracies that administer them, so that anyone below a certain income
for whatever reason would get a cheque.

KR: Yeah, there is now a $5-billion dollar surplus in the govern-
ment's U.I. coffers which a lot of people can't access because of the
tighter restrictions. And the surplus is projected to reach more
than $9 billion in the following fiscal year. There should be some
public debate about what we do with that money. The Right has
proposed workfare as an answer to the problems of joblessness
and what they call dependence on welfare. Soon they'll be saying:
"Hey, you woman at home, even if you have young children, if
you're able-bodied, you're employable. We can stick you out there
and exploit you." But maybe it's actually better for that woman to
be with her child, raising her child, because the work she's doing
in that context is more meaningful and valuable to society as a
whole and probably more fulfilling, even though you do have to
deal with the issue of women feeling trapped and isolated at home.

What are we saying as a society if we agree that it's okay to take low-income mothers, or anyone for that matter, and force them into the work force, while a smaller class of women are made to "babysit" the children?

JR: Society should recognize that parents staying home with their kids in their first year or two, if the parents so choose, would be a good thing for society. Some Scandinavian countries provide well-paid parental leave for one or two years for either parent. But we should make it a collective choice, rather than singling out those people who are forced to choose between working full time or being on welfare. That's the kind of thing we have to think through in terms of social policy. I know there are some feminist academics working on this issue now, and I think it's absolutely central.

Clearly we have to oppose workfare. We have to create real jobs for people and take away this moralist approach to welfare. I had a guy on my TV show, a homeless guy who had just gotten a subsidized apartment, and he put it very eloquently. He said: "It costs $6,000 for me to be on welfare, it costs $18,000 for me to be in a shelter and it costs $70,000 for me to be in jail. Now, what makes more sense for society?" In Ontario, and I assume it's the same in Alberta, they are throwing people off the welfare rolls and people are winding up in these shelters. Even in B.C. they are refusing welfare to those who have been in the province less than three months. It's all costing a lot more public money, but it doesn't show up in the same place in the budget, so politicians can pander to public attitudes of blaming the poor. It's really terrible.

KR: The current approach is really not even about being fiscally responsible. It's about punishing people for being poor, blaming them for poverty. It returns us to that bizarre and archaic notion of the survival of the fittest. Just work hard and you'll be fine.

JR: Take two groups: tax evaders or people who don't charge GST in the underground economy, and poor people "cheating" welfare, which might mean that recipients are living with a man or that they made a couple of extra bucks that week and didn't report it. Just compare the government's attitude towards those two groups, and you see that it's nothing to do with economics.

KR: Metro Council in Toronto has just adopted a proposal to fingerprint all welfare recipients, even though the research shows that fraud made up 0.5 per cent of the 1995 welfare budget. Obviously fraud is not good, but it will probably cost more to set this whole system up than the city will save in catching defrauders. We shouldn't forget what these policies are doing to people. Welfare snitch lines don't uplift the human spirit.

Economic arguments are abstract, but we can all see that food banks are going begging while commercial banks are swelling with profit and hoarding wealth. There needs to be a social movement, one that includes labour, community groups and the faith community, that puts a human face on all this.

JR: One of the questions long-time anti-poverty activist Jean Swanson asks is, "Why is it that with a certain group of people, poor people, we think we have to take away money to get them to work, while with other people, CEOs of corporations, we have to give them more and more money in order to get them to work?"

I agree with you that our social movements have to expose the values behind the agenda of the Right. We need a few simple economic and social ideas combined with a campaign on values. Of course, in the area of work, the attacks on labour standards, union rights, pay and employment equity, and public services must be resisted as well. But my view is that resistance without alternatives cannot and will not succeed.

KR: I think we need to encourage and defend unionization, which is the major tool we have to deal with corporate power. The other thing is that, on a global scale, the work force is increasingly non-white, young and female—three groups that have traditionally been most exploited. To revitalize and stay relevant, some resources have to be given to a diverse group of unionists to organize unorganized workers of colour, women and youth of all communities. Some have said that companies should be forced to disclose any changes in the number of workers they employ here and abroad. One good thing the Harris government did was to disclose the names and salaries of all public servants who make more than $100,000. I think that the salaries of CEOs and upper management in the private sector should be publicized as well, to build pressure for salary caps and progressive taxation.

Right-wing Canadian politicians have regular meetings with their neo-con American buddies to swap stories and strategies. We need to have more connections with workers and anti-poverty activists in the States and worldwide. And to keep documenting what is happening to people on welfare. Self-employment and small business co-ops are something to look at, even though this approach has its limits. But we have to remember that we're dealing with a structural problem. If you tie a standard of living to paid work alone, then some people will always be losers, because they can't get paid work or because how well they live depends on what bosses feel is enough pay. So long-term solutions mean changing to an economy based not on profit but on sharing resources.

JR: I agree. I have been a socialist most of my adult life. But I think we need more concrete strategies today. I think a campaign for a shorter work week combined with a liveable guaranteed annual income is a good place to start in terms of dealing with the insecurities and inequalities at work. The labour movement was born in the struggle for the eight-hour day, and there is no reason why the broad social movement you speak about can't be organized around a different vision of society, where work and wealth are shared more equitably. There are small steps that can be taken along the way. The new employment standards act in B.C., for example, which provides family responsibility leave, protection for domestic workers and new rules on flexible work schedules, is a step in the right direction.

4

A Place of Belonging

· ·

IDENTITY POLITICS

KR: There are so many muddled notions out there about identity politics. The Right and the Left both see identity politics as a problem, but for different reasons. The Right says identity politics is bad because it leads to creating "special" rights for different groups. The Left argues against identity politics because it's "divisive." They think that focussing too much on being a woman or being Black forgets class politics, forgets, for example, that there are white men who are also poor. Both these critiques come together in agreeing that the white male should not be displaced, although of course they don't actually say that.

To me, identity politics is about marginalized people fighting for their rights and to be themselves. Women, people of colour and others have been wronged just because of who they are. In Canada, aboriginal children were forced into residential schools where they were stripped of their culture and separated from their families and communities. Women across the board continue to be paid less than men. Women with disabilities face the highest levels of job discrimination and poverty. And gays and lesbians are sometimes disowned by their families and get attacked in the streets. These are just a few examples.

If the critics of identity politics understood history, they would see that one of the first things an oppressor does to subjugate someone is to take away that person's identity. For me the most dramatic moment of *Roots*, the TV program about slavery, was when they took an enslaved African man and asked him, "What is your name?" And he said, "My name is Kunta Kinte." And they kept beating him until he said that his name was Toby and took on the slave master's name. That's how you break a people's spirit. You take away their identity, you take away the things that make them whole people: their language, history, culture, spirituality. What identity politics does is try to reclaim what is lost, so that not only do you feel like a whole, valuable human being but you understand that your identity is not the oppressor's identity. Your issues and concerns are not the same as the issues and concerns of your slave master. You don't have the same values as the person who is keeping you down. You start to realize the source of your power, and your strength is what has been hidden from you, what has been denied to you. It's the moment that you realize you're not at fault. You didn't do something wrong. That's what is threatening.

When women of colour fight for their rights, everyone benefits. It doesn't hurt anyone. I challenge anyone to show me how Black women fighting for their rights actually denies someone else's rights. The history of Black people in this part of the world has been one of fighting for fairness, for fair employment practices, fair housing, human rights bodies. All of those things came out of the civil rights movement, and everyone has benefited from them.

JR: I think you make a good point about identity. If you read some of the liberal writers on this topic, like Robert Fulford or Richard Gwyn, they tend to say, "We used to be much more united in this country, we used to have a common identity." Of course the common identity was *their* identity as white Anglo males. Things were much more united when white Anglo males defined reality and everyone else had to fit into that. The struggle to define a new reality not constructed by the white male patriarchy is inevitably a struggle where there is going to be conflict. You talk about being forced to identify with the oppressor. I could put it in other language: that you have to fit in. So if you're a woman and you want to be a lawyer, you have to wear a suit, act like a man, be willing to work sixty hours a week, and so on. If you want to be a woman politician, you have to act like a male politician. For many years society has been constructed so that the only way you could succeed was to identify with the elite, with the dominant class, with the well-to-do white Anglo male. What identity politics is fundamentally about, I agree with you, is saying, "No, we are not doing that any more. We have a right to be who we are and to be recognized for who we are, whether we're Black people, or women, or gays and lesbians. You don't have to adopt our reality, but you do have to recognize it." That's what the struggle for same-sex benefits is about, the fight for parental and family leave, the struggle for aboriginal self-government and the struggle to change curriculum. They are all about recognizing the contributions of women and people of colour.

I think identity politics is also about belonging. I know I have often felt that I didn't belong in society. It's a common experience among people who feel marginalized. In my case it's not so much being Jewish as being female and trying to rebel against the role that was set up for me as female. I always felt weird, like something was wrong with me, something was different about me. What identity politics gives you is a way to say, this is my group, the group that I belong to. I am part of this. And that's very empowering for people.

But I think that if identity politics is taken to an extreme, it *can* hurt other people, because then it can be exclusive. In the women's movement, I've heard people say that you can only speak legitimately if you are part of this group or that group. I don't think that's what the majority of feminists believe, although we are branded by it. But I have seen that kind of dynamic.

KR: I think we should take this on right away. This is another mixed-up notion I keep on hearing, that somehow identity politics means that if you're from the dominant group then you can't speak out against the oppression. If you're white, you can't talk about racism. If you're straight, you can't talk about homophobia. I think that's totally wrong. I think it gets confused with the notion of speaking *for* another group. I want more white people to speak up against racism. It gets really tiring for us to be the only ones to speak out about it. But what you cannot do if you want to be an ally is to speak for other people. You can't say how other people should conduct their struggles or what they should be doing. You shouldn't try to dictate to them. But that's very different from speaking out against the barriers those people face.

JR: I think that's a distinction people don't understand. I'll use the example of the musical *Showboat*. The Black community in Toronto opposed the production of *Showboat* because they considered the play to be racist. I didn't necessarily agree with them.

But in a talk I gave to the United Way, I argued that whether or not the organization agreed with the Black community about *Showboat*, they shouldn't have done what they did, used a performance as a fund-raiser, out of respect for the community's position. As a white person I have to say, "Maybe I don't agree with this position, but a lot of the people I respect in the Black community are supporting it, so either I'm going to be neutral or I'm going to side with the Black community." And that's something I think people have a very hard time with. They think you're being terrorized by political correctness, or that you're saying because someone is Black they are right. That's not what I'm saying. I am saying that as a white person I may not fully appreciate the concerns being expressed. I can raise my concerns, but it would take a lot for me to publicly oppose the Black community on an issue like this.

But all that being said, I didn't agree with the Black community. *Showboat* is a historical thing and it's a musical. I don't think it should be censored or banned.

KR: There was never a censorship issue here. The demand of the protesters was not that the show be banned outright but that it be boycotted and that schoolchildren not be taken to see it on any "educational" field trips. *Showboat* is a gross distortion of the reality and brutality of the conditions African-Americans lived under at the time the play is set in. The Black characters are portrayed as happy, shuffling, singing buffoons. *Showboat* rewrites history. As with *Miss Saigon*, the history of struggle, suffering, genocide and resistance is obliterated.

JR: A lot of Black people in the States don't agree, though. Certainly, by today's standards the show is racist. But art reflects the society of the time. Do we then change it because we find it objectionable now? There are issues around art and culture and freedom of expression, and changing or rewriting history.

KR: "Art" can also be used to tell lies, to indoctrinate people, to glorify one people while denigrating another. M. Nourbese Philip deals with all these issues really well in her book *Showing Grit.* "Art" can be just propaganda that justifies everything that's going on in this society. As far as *Showboat* goes, we're living in Canada, and we have a different Black population here, one that comes from majority countries in the Caribbean and Africa, so we have a different relationship to and understanding of the issues.

The African-Canadian community is very aware of the fact that racism does not only express itself through police brutality or in being denied a job. We've fought racism on every single level: immigration, human rights issues, in the schools. But your soul and your psyche are also wounded when you're excluded from the art galleries, and when you're portrayed in museums only as a conquered, unintelligent people. What is the point of living today, and knowing what we know, if all we're going to do is perpetuate and glorify everything that was destructive to the human personality by saying uncritically, "It's historical"? The reality is that we're in an underclass, and we're seeing ourselves constantly being represented in ways that are negative and damaging.

Oppressed groups struggle around identity issues, but more white people should talk about how they experience themselves in the world as a group. We don't hear white people talking about what it means to them to be white. It's kind of disturbing that the only people who talk about being white are KKK people.

JR: People don't talk about being white because they don't identify as being white. I don't identify as being white. When I see a white woman running for political office, I don't identify with her on racial grounds. I wouldn't vote for her because she's white, but I might vote for her because she's a woman. If you're part of the dominant group, you don't consciously identify as part of that group, because that's the dominant reality.

KR: Yeah, I've heard white men identifying as "just human beings." The whole society is dominated by white people, so the power becomes invisible to them.

I was struck by what Katie Rich, the Innu chief, said when she was talking about the low-level military flights that NATO conducts over Innu land: that military people justify these actions by saying, "Well, no one lives there." This is how Native people are treated, as nonexistent or not human. It was the same experience for Africans with slavery. People don't realize that slavery also existed in Canada and was only abolished in 1834. Africans were reduced to commodities to be bought and sold. Understanding that is a place of beginning, because only then can you start to understand other larger or more contemporary questions.

But white people have a particular history, just like all people have a particular history, and Europeans have particular ethnicities. When you don't recognize that, it leads into these weird ideas I've read in some recent books that Canada doesn't have a culture, or that our culture is "caring and sharing and being tolerant." That's not a culture. Those are specific qualities that human beings have or don't have. We do have a dominant culture. It's Anglo culture. People who come here, even other European people, have to fit into that culture. Being white means they can fit in better. Nobody ever talks about that. Nobody talks about the fact that we still live in a colonial place. We still have a Queen of England reigning over us. If you want to become a Canadian citizen, you have to swear allegiance to the queen, her heirs and successors. We haven't even graduated to being fully independent yet.

JR: I don't agree with you there. I think Canada's independent and the Queen's just a symbol.

KR: But she's a symbol of oppression, a symbol of slavery, a symbol of genocide to the Native people. Which connects to another point. A lot of people think identity politics is based on the glorification of victimization. This notion is very wrong. When we recall slavery, when we recall that genocide, we are accused of trying to say that this historical suffering makes us better than other people. Or even more strangely, that somehow we've been advantaged by the fact that we've gone through all this pain and terror. When we recall these things, people say, "Oh, that happened so long ago," or "That's not the reality today." But we're still experiencing the fallout of that history. White people haven't recognized that slavery is not just about Black people. We talk about Black History Month, but in reality that history is also world history. It's just as important for white people to understand how their ancestors enslaved Africans as it is for Black people to understand how their ancestors were enslaved. History shows us the source of our divisions. These divisions haven't come from people claiming their identity, but from the suppression of it. We've been physically and legally prevented from working together. The last officially segregated school in Canada didn't close until 1965.

JR: I think looking at the source of divisions is important. One of the things that always gets said is that identity politics is divisive. My answer to that is that discrimination is divisive. Identity politics is an attempt to deal with that discrimination. There's nothing perverse about people identifying with a particular group. Your analysis is that it's historical, and I agree that's true, but I also think you identify with a group because you face discrimination as part of that group. So if I identify with women, it's because I'm treated like a woman. I was denied jobs when I was young because I was a woman, I was sexually harassed because I was a woman, and I've been reminded most of my life that whatever I wanted to do, being a woman was a disadvantage.

Sometimes I think we make a mistake by arguing a case based primarily on history. If the discrimination was not continuing today, we would have no need for anti-discrimination measures. I don't know how many times I've heard the argument against employment equity legislation that we don't need it because time will overcome the historical discrimination. The problem is not only historical; it's also current. That's why people identify in these groups, why they're listed in the charter and in the human rights code. These are the groups that face discrimination in various systematic ways. It comes out of history, but it still exists today.

There are times when people in our movements do become caricatures in the way that critics of identity politics suggest. I'll give you an example. About ten years ago at a NAC annual general meeting, before the term "identity politics" came into the lexicon, there was a major policy resolution on prostitution. The resolution was written by a committee of prostitutes and their allies, and among other things it said that pimping could be a positive alternative lifestyle. Now, I didn't know anything about issues around prostitution, but I knew damn well that I wasn't going to vote for anything that said pimping was a positive alternative lifestyle. I got up and said, "Look, maybe I'm ignorant of these issues, but to me pimping is exploitative of women, and I'm not going to vote for this." Then someone from a prostitutes' rights group got up and laid a guilt trip about it and said how we middle-class women didn't understand that prostitutes' live-in girlfriends or boy-friends were often busted for pimping. Well, fine, let's put that in the resolution, but that's different from saying that pimping can be positive. Afterwards, people came up to me and said, "Judy, you're so courageous." If it was so wrong, why didn't other people get up? But until I spoke, the sentiment was, if the prostitutes want us to vote for this, then we have to vote for this. So even way back then, before racism was a central issue in NAC, before even lesbian rights was up front as an issue, that kind of notion was there in the women's movement. If the group directly involved says something is correct, then it is correct. This seems to me an over-correction in answer to a society that doesn't listen to people at all.

And there is still among some people in the women's movement the idea that you can't challenge a person if they're speaking from their own experience. I certainly agree that a Black woman knows better than I do what it means to be Black in this society, but that doesn't mean she can't be wrong about something, even something to do with racism. In the women's movement there has often been guilt around that stuff.

KR: It's bad when people go along with something even when they don't agree with it. It's also bad when people preface their remarks by saying, "As a Black . . ." or "As a lesbian . . ." and then go on to put out their position as if being Black or lesbian means that their position is automatically correct. This makes it seem that if you disagree with their position you are racist, homophobic or otherwise bigoted. That shuts down debate. And one of the problems we have in some movements is that we haven't engaged in enough debate or dialogue on certain issues. So we lose skills around how to be critical and how to debate issues.

JR: True. When conflicts based in racism or homophobia don't get dealt with, then sometimes the situation will polarize based on identity politics, and it can become destructive. In my experience, the responsibility has usually been with the dominant group not responding to the real concerns of the other group.

There there is also an issue around class politics. I think we have focussed our energy in the last period, in the women's movement in particular, on gender, race and sexual orientation, but we don't talk enough about class issues. We do understand the concept of multiple oppression, but we don't recognize it in class terms. And more and more, those issues are coming to the fore. Social division and class issues. I think the alliance the women's movement has built with the labour movement and with anti-poverty groups has to become stronger. The NAC/Canadian Labour Congress Women's March against Poverty last spring was a good example of the kind of coalition-building we need at a grass-roots level. Just as there was an invisibility of oppression based on gender and race until we had a women's movement and a civil rights movement, in Canada there's really been an invisibility of class. The social consensus we've had for the last generation, which meant that working people could get a share of the good life, has broken down. Now the business class is waging war on working-class and poor people, and we have to start talking in those terms. It's hard to do that in Canada. It's a new challenge for us.

KR: Yeah, everyone thinks we're all middle class. I agree class issues are very important, especially now. This country has to break out of denial. Racism is also intensifying here, yet so many people continue to claim it's not a problem in Canada.

JR: I agree. I think in addition to areas like restrictive immigra-tion laws, stereotyped media portrayals of people of colour and

the backlash against employment equity, we can see it in the public reaction to some cultural issues. White people are generally
feeling a loss of control because of the economic situation, but
they get hung up on symbolic things like Sikhs wanting to wear
turbans in the R.C.M.P. or in the Legion hall. Those kinds of
struggles both come out of racism and fuel the fires of racism.

KR: The experience of Chinese people in this country is a good
example of how immigration policy changes depending on the
circumstances. In the early 1800s Canada wanted Chinese men to
work on the railroads. But when there were "too many" Chinese
living in Canada, the federal government imposed a head tax as a
way to keep them out. Today, the government has set up offices in
Hong Kong so they can lure wealthy Chinese people into the
country and get them to invest their money here.

JR: And now there's a backlash to that. In Vancouver and
Toronto, there's a backlash against wealthy immigrants of colour,
particularly Chinese people but also some South Asian immigrants. I read a story in the paper about some white people in B.C.
moving out of their wealthy neighbourhood because too many
Chinese people were moving in. A lot of cultural tensions are
emerging, and I think this kind of racism is developing a character similar to that of anti-Semitism.

KR: Why do you say that?

JR: Well, hatred of Jews has often been based on resentment
of the success of Jews. Hitler painted Jews as vermin, but he was
also able to create resentment against them because many
German Jews were merchants or bankers. In some Black communities in the States, there's anti-Semitism because Jews used to

live in those communities and were the business owners and the landlords.

KR: There are tensions between people of African descent and European Jewish people, but also creative possibilities. We've both gone through holocausts, and we see the world in a very different way than other people do. We have a continual tradition of resistance in both our cultures. When I think about what a non-racist Canada would look like, or what I hope for or expect for African-Canadians in this country, I think of the example of Jewish people, and how Jewish people have been able to maintain their culture and institutions, like Hebrew schools, but also integrate into the broader society and excel. I think that's where some of the tensions have come in, in fact, because while Jewish people and African people have been allies in many ways, because of white skin many Jewish people have been able to move to another level of society and don't necessarily always continue that same tradition of struggle.

JR: That's true, certainly recently. But the Jews in Nazi Germany were more assimilated than Jews in Canada today, and yet when a Fascist government came in and decided to use anti-Semitism as a way of consolidating its power, it didn't matter how assimilated you were: you were still Jewish. It's like when I, along with twelve prominent Jews in Toronto, got a live bullet in the mail a couple of years ago. Even though I don't identify much as a Jew, to the Nazis in Toronto I'm a Jew, and that's all that matters to them about me.

I agree with you that Jews have been able to integrate and assimilate. I don't think anti-Semitism is the same as racism. I don't think anti-Semitism affects me the way racism affects you. I'm not oppressed as a Jew, and I don't think Jews in North

America are oppressed as Jews. We have access to everything. There are no barriers to me because I'm Jewish, and there haven't been in my generation. My parents' generation experienced that, but I didn't. But it's also true that the residue of anti Semitism is always there I'll give you an example. It's very rarely recognized that a lot of the white people who do stand up against racism are Jewish Like Stephen Lewis, who wrote a report two years ago on racism in Ontario. And yet when Garth Drabinsky produced *Showboat*, he was immediately identified as Jewish. That to me is an example of anti-Semitism. If a Jew does something progressive he's not recognized as a Jew, but if he does something reactionary, then it's said, "Why are you doing something reactionary or racist? You're Jewish, and you shouldn't do that."

KR: I think some of the conflict comes from the higher expectations we have of each other. I remember when I was a student at McGill University and the *McGill Daily* put out an issue on anti-racism that included a controversial article on Palestinian politics. Everything exploded. The Black Student Network and Jewish students at McGill had a meeting, and people said they felt that the low point Black-Jewish relations had reached in the States was affecting things here in Canada. So there was a conversation about what our relationship had been, both positive and negative. The complaint around *Showboat* was that a Jewish person should not have written or produced this show because they should understand our pain.

JR: The reality is that the vast majority of Jews chose to integrate into mainstream society. To the extent that I identify with Judaism, it's with the strain of Jews who fought oppression, who were radical, who were part of the civil rights movement. I think most Jewish feminists identify with that history of the Jewish people. But the reality is, even though when you look at the Left you'll still see a higher than normal proportion of Jews, the mainstream of the Jewish community has moved way to the right. In the States and Canada now you actually have right-wing Jews. David Frum is an example. Very prominent members of the Right are Jewish, which you rarely would have seen even in my parents' generation.

KR: In a different way, African-Canadians are trying to integrate and make a better living, but it doesn't seem to be working for a lot of us. The larger society continues to deny us opportunities and discriminate against us. Immigration laws change to keep us out. Police and the criminal justice system are bearing down on African-Canadian youth. And the school system is failing them.

Where we do "succeed," the price of that social integration is often giving up our culture and weakening our commitment to social justice. We see who gets rewarded and we know that, in this society, people of colour are successful to the extent that we assimilate into white culture and do things that are productive for white culture but not necessarily for us. We still have to fight racism and hold our governments accountable for their actions. But we also have to ask on whose terms we "integrate" into that broader society. What do we gain or lose in the process? How will we survive these difficult times as a community? I think these are real questions for African-Canadians now, because we're seeing a lot of the institutions we've created to redress wrongs and protect our rights being undermined. The human rights commissions are not even helping us to fight pure discrimination. It leads us to think that we have to come up with other alternatives. And the other alternatives seem to be "doing for self" and supporting our own businesses, returning to build up our own community. We're seeing a greater sense of alienation from mainstream society among Black people.

JR: But isn't the alternative really to transform society, so that your culture becomes part of the culture of the society in a significant way? Isn't that the true meaning of multiculturalism? A truly multicultural society would be one in which African culture, Chinese culture and so on would be an integral part of the culture of our country that we could all appreciate and learn from. If you look at Brazil or Cuba, for example, the African culture is so central to the culture of those societies that, even though Black people aren't a majority, they're a significant portion of society.

KR: But there is still an intense level of racism in Brazil. In North America, people of African descent have made our presence felt in music and sports, where we are allowed to excel. But we still don't control the music industry, we don't own the sports teams. Culture is also about money and power and being able to control your destiny. I'm not advocating some kind of simplistic separatism. I'm just suspicious of an "integration" unaccompanied by a recognition of our history and a genuine sharing of power.

JR: Still, isn't the solution not to have all these separate groups taking care of themselves but rather to develop a culture that is a combination of cultures, an intermixture of cultures? I think there are elements of that now. Toronto is a much more vibrant and rich city because of the different cultures here. When Americans come to Toronto, they always notice all the cultures that maintain a distinct identity. But somehow we have to get beyond the restaurant and tourist attraction part, which is the level we've got to now. We have to explore how to transform things so that no one culture is dominant.

5

The Next Stage

. . . .

CANADIAN FEMINISM

KR: The term "feminism" keeps travelling through a revolving door of meaning, so I'd like to start by defining it. To me, feminism is about men and women sharing power equally. And so it necessarily transforms the world for the better for women *and* men. If women change, men have to change too. And we're still in that process of change. We've won the right to vote, but we don't run the country. We've got two women Supreme Court justices, but more and more women are living in poverty. There's a feeling that women can do anything we want, but we're still harassed on the job, paid less than men, ignored by history. And the list goes on. There's the famous cigarette ad that targets women with the slogan "You've come a long way, baby." Recently I saw a young woman wearing a T-shirt that said, "We haven't come far enough. And don't call me baby."

Feminism has always gotten a bad rap in mainstream society,

but the difference today is that there's money to be made from the dissing. We've seen a rash of books and articles about "the feminists" who squander taxpayer dollars to fund our pet projects while we work tirelessly to champion victimhood. And we're still dealing with the nonsense that feminism is dead, bankrupt or irrelevant. The fiction that feminism has run its course.

With all these attacks, it's no surprise that feminists get defensive, but we need to get critical and strategic, too. We've got to do a better job at countering the conservative claptrap. And we shouldn't let a right-wing climate shut down open and honest debate about the state of our movement.

Women still really need organized feminism, especially in this time of backlash. And there are some important questions we should be asking. How do we encourage the leadership and participation of a whole new generation of women? How do we deal with the cutbacks that are shutting our organizations down?

JR: I agree that those are important questions. While it is certainly true that women have made enormous strides in the past generation, it is also true that gender oppression is still very much with us. And while some well-educated, professional single women have come close to achieving economic equality, limits on reproductive freedom, lack of affordable child care, violence against women and the glass ceiling—the male domination of politics, industry and academia—persist. When we look at women who face additional barriers, whether because of race, social class, sexual orientation or disability, there is more inequality. On the international level, women are just beginning to make progress. Feminists have never looked only at the issue of women's inequality. From the suffragists who fought for social programs to the modern-day feminist movement, which has been part of every progressive struggle, whether to improve pensions or save medicare, feminism has always been about improving the quality of life for everyone in society. And today, women's groups are involved in a broader series of issues than ever before. That's why I find these attacks on feminism as male-bashing so bizarre. The women's movement in Canada, and from what I can see internationally, has never been more closely aligned with other movements for social change, like the labour movement, the anti-racist movement, the Third World solidarity movements, what have you, all of which include men.

KR: Well, that's the thing about the backlash arguments: they're illogical. If feminists concentrate strictly on fighting for our own rights, then we're accused of ignoring or hating men, but when we focus on labour, the economy or war, then we're accused of dividing women, because inevitably these issues divide women politically.

JR: When you're fighting for social change, you're always vilified. Students have sometimes asked me why we insist on using the word "feminist" when feminism has such negative connotations in the mainstream media. I tell them that we didn't used to call ourselves feminists, we used to call ourselves the women's liberation movement. Then our critics called us "women's libbers," so we changed the name. But it's not the name, it's the struggle for equality that is being vilified.

The inequality of women is structural. It is embedded in the system. And unless you transform the system, then what happens is what is happening in Canada today. When there are cuts they hit women hardest, because women are at the bottom of the barrel. They hit people of colour and women hardest.

KR: And of course the cutbacks will hit poor and working-class women hardest of all. I think the tensions that exist in the women's movement today have to do not only with our struggles to make our organizations inclusive of all women but with figuring out what our starting point for action should be. We're moving from asking to be included in the system to saying the system has to change.

JR: In the 1980s, the women's movement focussed on what I call single issues. There was a pro-choice movement, a child-care movement, an anti-violence movement, an employment equity movement. What is happening now, with globalization, with the rise of neo-conservatism, with the economic attacks we have been under, is that it's become clear you can't just fight on single issues. You have to look at the overall picture. I think most feminists understand that now.

KR: I don't agree. A lot of privileged women are just now grappling with this idea of feminism as an all-encompassing kind of politic, with understanding that oppressions are interconnected. Global structural adjustment programs, continued militarization, the unequal distribution of power: all these are tied to sexism and racism. Feminists of colour have been saying this for years. But this idea is still very much under attack. I've heard people claim that in looking at the big picture, women's specific, everyday issues and struggles will get lost. I have always argued that looking at the big picture is the only way to find ourselves, to know how we fit in it. To say that feminism speaks to a broad range of issues is not to dilute feminism but to acknowledge how multifaceted it is, or ought to be.

JR: I actually think liberal feminism, the idea that you can just change some rules and achieve equality, is dead in the women's movement. But there are women who were once active feminists who now are part of and identify with the elites. They often attack the women's movement as being too narrow. What they really mean is that they don't feel represented any more, and they feel conflicted about that. But a lot of feminists in the North who maybe ten years ago were talking about how getting more women MPs or senators or CEOs would achieve equality are not talking like that any more. The women's movement is getting more radical, and this is true internationally. When I was at the UN NGO Forum on Women in Huairou, none of the plenary speeches focussed on what we would call women's issues. They all addressed the global economic agenda and the rise of the Right, the rise of fundamentalism and the need for the women's movement to present an alternative for humanity.

KR: But knowing that achieving equality is more complex makes it harder to organize. I was talking to a woman the other day who first got involved in the abortion rights movement. As she pointed out, the urgency of the issue was clear, and the enemies to abortion rights were known. But when you understand the enemy is the way the whole system works, where do you start?

JR: A very interesting question. In the sixties, we also believed the enemy was the system. At first there were the clear demands of the civil rights struggle and the anti-war struggle, but then it became obvious that the "establishment," as we called it then, did not want to change. So we got more radical. "Smash the State" and "Burn Baby Burn" were the kinds of slogans American radicals used. In Canada we were more polite, of course, but we really believed that we, the youth, would make the revolution in a couple of years. It took me until practically 1980 to give up on the idea that revolutionary change was just around the corner.

I think one of the strengths of your generation is that you are not so naive. But maybe that sophistication leads to a certain paralysis, too.

KR: I think there are a number of factors that affect how young women feel about feminism. One obvious thing is the negative media portrayal of feminism. But it's more than that. The success of the feminist movement means that a lot of the most obvious forms of sexism have been eliminated. At one time, for example, women were actually barred from entering law school. Today, women make up 50 per cent of law students. But after graduation, women are still hired less often by law firms and they have a harder time sustaining a practice. The gains we've made make some people feel that we don't need feminism any more. But the fact is that while some women are doing quite well, many more still face barriers. Often less obvious barriers, which makes the struggle trickier. At the same time, for women who do understand the need for feminism, it's hard to find a way to get actively involved. We've been bombarded with messages of materialism and individualism and there's a disconnection from any tradition of struggle.

JR: As far as your last point goes, that was even more true for my generation. When I was growing up, I had no idea of any mass movement for social change until the civil rights movement became visible. I knew nothing of suffragists or even the workers' movement in the 1930s. I actually think that the continuity of struggle now might be the problem. When I was young, I didn't have to answer to so many older people involved in the same struggle. I could do my own thing, make my own mistakes.

KR: Yes, there is real exclusion sometimes. About a year ago, a friend told me that young women who wanted to get involved in organizing an event for International Women's Day were turned away with the excuse that the organizing was by invitation only. When I was seventeen, I went to a NAC annual general meeting with a friend. She got up the courage to speak in one of the sessions. She said something kind of naive and was laughed down by the older women there. She was pretty upset by that, and it didn't exactly encourage her to get involved. On the other hand, I might not have gone on to become more active if older women hadn't encouraged me.

JR: Cliquism and impatience with new people are general problems, but obviously they have a worse effect on young people.

KR: There's a mutual mistrust and lack of respect that happens sometimes between older and younger women. In the women's movement, older women have said, "Listen, young thing, I've been doing this for years," in a dismissive way. And in the popular culture, and the book world, young feminists who diss our elders are promoted and touted as cutting edge, even though their critiques do not advance feminist thought. Both kinds of behaviour are a waste of time and pull us away from the source of our power.

Young women have to develop and run our own organizations. It's one of the few ways we can gain leadership skills and talk together. But I think it's crucial that once leadership emerges from younger women, older women encourage and mentor them.

Another thing is that a lot of young women's activism is in the realm of culture. If you produce a magazine or a video or host a show on community radio, there's something tangible and immediate about it. One of the challenges we face is to create new organizations where young women will feel that they can have an effect on changing society.

JR: One of the things we understood in the sixties and seventies was the importance of organizing. Everyone who was active was involved in movement building, meaning building organizations, organizing campaigns, reaching out to new people, organizing meetings, teach-ins, demonstrations, and so on. What that did was give individuals a way to get involved. Now, I think partly because of the sophistication of our existing organizations, most of which had their roots in those days, young people don't see a place where they can make a difference.

KR: The success of the women's movement has led it away from that kind of grassroots organizing. There are very few "entry points" to feminism if you're isolated and don't have friends who are interested in women's issues. A lot of psychological barriers still need to be broken through about being smart and independent, liking your body, thinking critically and speaking up. I think we need to get back to consciousness-raising groups, to meeting together on a regular basis to discuss where we go from here. Young women are obviously concerned about the seemingly jobless future we face. There are young mothers struggling to cope with the demands of parenthood. Teen-age girls sometimes feel pressured to have sex when they're not ready or might be confused about their sexual identities. Last year, I met a whole bunch of young women refugees from Africa, many of whom had fled civil war in their homelands and are having to deal with death in their families or haven't been able to contact family members, and at the same time they are just coping with the culture shock and feelings of isolation. Why don't we meet around these issues? Real issues. I think there is a need for older women to do that too. So we can figure out how we are going to support each other through the changes we're experiencing.

JR: It's true. We've stopped talking to each other about our life experiences. And at the beginning of the second wave of feminism, it was those discussions that empowered us. Consciousness-raising groups may be part of the answer, but I do think we have to start organizing again.

KR: How do we redefine feminist struggle in this new climate? Many of our issues have gotten professionalized along the way. And while we have been grappling more in the women's movement with questions around race, there is a whole class component that I think we still only pay lip service to. We talk about the "feminization of poverty," but we haven't really strategized around combatting it.

JR: There is also the problem of movements getting co-opted. You start with the raw organizing power. You start with the abortion caravan and women chaining themselves to the balcony of the House of Commons, or you start with an alternate women's constitutional conference, or with women applying for jobs in a steel plant, or with women working with immigrant women. But the problem has been, as soon as you get to the point where the government starts to recognize that they have to deal with the issue, a process of co-option begins. The result is, as you say, the professionalization of our issues, dressing them up in language and demands that government bureaucrats, politicians and the media can accept. So our slogans change from "Free abortion on demand" to "Freedom of choice." Our demands change from affirmative action to employment equity, and our tactics change from using the streets to relying on committee rooms.

I think what has kept us from getting too co-opted as a movement is the struggle of various women for inclusion. Lesbians have really led the way. Lesbians have always been a significant group within the women's movement. They were involved in fights on every issue from abortion to equal pay, even when the issue didn't directly affect them. But for a long time mainstream women's groups didn't want to recognize the contributions of lesbians for fear of being labelled as a bunch of male-hating dykes. I remember being shocked to hear from lesbians on the NAC executive that right into the 1980s they felt they had to remain closeted to retain their credibility. But lesbians fought for visibility, and I think they succeeded in forcing groups like NAC to openly acknowledge their contributions to the movement and to strongly support their issues.

KR: NAC still has a way to go on lesbian issues. Some women do not feel it is vocal enough in supporting gay and lesbian struggles. And other women's groups are grappling with these issues too. At the Congress of Black Women's national meeting in 1994, one of the delegates, who is an open lesbian, was approached by her chapter to run for president. She decided to accept the nomination and put her name on the ballot. She had a lot of support and thought she would win, until another delegate announced her candidacy just before the vote. An emergency meeting was called, and the lesbian candidate was directly told by a few of the delegates that they could not support a lesbian as national president. It was a difficult experience, but this incident led to some open and honest discussion about how to address and overcome homophobia. I think there is greater awareness and more willingness among many members now to look at how homophobia divides us, and to put an end to that.

JR: Things have become very complicated in the current economic climate. The Liberal welfare state that works to co-opt our movements is disappearing, and we don't know what is going to take its place. I think we are being pushed back to the days before we had attention paid to our issues. Back to the days of grassroots organizing. We need more ways to involve women in action. I'm hoping that the Women's March against Poverty will spur groups of women across the country to continue organizing around the issues. Or, as I have argued for years, that NAC will develop a mechanism which allows individual members to join, not just women's groups, so that there can be NAC chapters across the country.

KR: Another issue we have to look at is how we are going to sustain and support women's organizations. Already we've lost Studio D, the National Film Board unit that produced films by and about women, and the DisAbled Women's Network, and other centres have had to close their doors. And we need to reexamine the whole issue of government funding. Getting money from government has implications. In some ways I think we haven't really understood that organizations like NAC, the National Organization of Immigrant and Visible Minority Women and other groups were formed in response to federal government initiatives. So the government "helped" to organize women and to contain women's agenda. We need to be more aware of constraints or of compromises that were made.

JR: I agree with you that government funding, especially at the national level, was designed to structure the women's movement in a way that government could relate to or control, depending on your point of view. That's why national women's groups tend to be more conservative than grassroots women's groups. But overall, I think government funding is one of the reasons why the women's movement in Canada is so strong. NAC, for example, was formed in opposition to what the government wanted. But it got government funding, and without it, I don't see how it could have survived as a cross-country, representative women's organization. As a federation of women's groups, NAC is unique, and its existence has strengthened the rest of the women's movement.

KR: I disagree that NAC was created in opposition to the state. At the beginning, it was formed as a watchdog organization to monitor government activity on the Royal Commission on the Status of Women. For most of its life, NAC has been at least 80 per cent funded by government. But today, only about 20 per cent of NAC's budget comes from the feds. I think that is a good thing, because the less feminists rely on government, the more self-determining—and critical of government—we can be. Of course there are pros and cons to funding. The Congress of Black Women has never had core government funding. It consciously sees itself as an advocacy group more than a service organization. Congress has made presentations to government and taken on many issues, including those of health care workers. They've done a lot of work and their voice isn't compromised, but no state funding has also meant it's difficult to maintain a permanent office in each region, and the Congress's political work means the organization can't get a charitable tax exemption for donations.

I think these hard times mean that women's groups are going to have to do more sharing, more co-operative work, to strengthen our bonds. We need to expand the definition of what feminist work is, too. The mainstream press and some women's studies texts have presented NAC as the voice of the feminist movement. Of course it is the largest feminist organization, but the movement has always occurred on different levels. For example, the Congress of Black Women hasn't fought only against racism. Congress women recently linked up with another group to establish a co-op housing complex. Sister Vision Press is celebrating ten successful years of publishing ground-breaking works by women of colour in Canada. The women of Camp Sisters in the Struggle are clearing land in the Ontario countryside and constructing buildings that will be permanent spaces for women's meetings and retreats. The Coalition of Visible Minority Women are teaching newcomers English, and Women Working with Immigrant Women are helping other organizations to assess women's needs, helping them to gain skills and to fight workplace sexism and discrimination. Low-income women are working on community economic development. You start to have a movement when women increasingly do things spontaneously to build community, like Women on Wheels, the young women travelling across Canada in a van handing out free books about women's lives. Like writer Dionne Brand giving free creative writing workshops for young Black women at a women's centre in Toronto. Like a friend of mine getting together with another woman to give free courses on feminism at a local alternative high school.

JR: The issue of economic independence is a crucial one. It is clear that advocacy groups can no longer rely on federal government funding, and it is questionable how long any service with a feminist approach will continue to receive funding in some provinces. I think women's groups here should do more of what they do in the U.S., selling certain goods and services as a way of fund-raising. NOW, the National Organization of Women in the U.S., does that, and some American gay and lesbian groups are doing it too. I personally have to buy lots of things. Why shouldn't I buy them from someone who is going to give 5 or 10 per cent of the money I spend to a women's group? There are many women like me, working-class women, middle-class women, who spend a lot of money and would like to spend it in a way that supports women's groups or other social change groups.

But there is a real resistance to doing this kind of thing in Canada. I guess women's groups are already so stretched that they don't want to invest time in a venture like this that may or may not reap rewards. No doubt the smaller market in Canada makes it a dicier proposition, too, but I still think it could work.

When you think about it, the women's movement has roots in every community and in every culture and in every country on the globe—it is truly a profound revolutionary movement. And it's not just women's organizations per se, but feminists organized inside every institution, like the women who have made our labour movement one of the most progressive in the world on equality rights, or a group of women executives I know in a famous hotel chain who have quietly organized to get their company to support a number of women's issues.

KR: We've been pretty successful on a lot of different levels, and yet we still feel frustration at not having some of our major demands met. We haven't made enough progress on things like child care or violence against women. Real understanding and change haven't seemed to root themselves deeply enough.

JR: Well, we've won major and fundamental reform: the legalization of abortion and equality rights in the charter, to name just two victories. In terms of why we have not had more success on child care, I think partly this comes out of the political culture. In Europe, where there is a culture that values social rights, women have had the most success on issues like child care and social programs to promote equality. In many places in Europe, there is a national child-care program. In North America, there is much more the notion of political rights and equality, so we have had the most success in the legal arena.

KR: North America has this "individual freedom" and "free choice" notion of equality.

JR: Right. Economic equality is understood to be essential to having equal rights in Europe, where there is much more of a sense of social entitlement. To get a national child-care program, particularly a non-profit, licenced child-care program, you also have to deal with the issue of women's role in the home.

This is where I think the feminist movement in North America has been weakest. We have attacked the sexual division of labour in the workplace. We have focussed a lot on economic equality in the workplace, reproductive freedom. We have focussed a lot on violence against women. These are all very important issues, but on the issue of the role of women inside the family, we have not done enough work. This is one reason why the social conservatives have had some success in appealing to women who work in the home. We haven't challenged men enough to take up parenting. The reality is that the high number of single-parent families *is* a problem. And it is a problem from a feminist point of view, because it is women who are carrying the burden of these families. Dead-beat dads are getting off scot-free, not only financially, which we have made an issue of, but emotionally and physically, right? I think it is bad for kids, too, not to have more than one adult role model. The third factor is money. A national child-care program would cost a lot of money. Free choice on abortion doesn't cost a bloody thing financially. Many of our gains have been in areas that don't cost the government a lot of money. And the Right has had some success in distorting our position on child care to make it seem that we are in favour of state-run creches, a kind of gulag for preschoolers.

But the most important impact of the women's movement, in my view, is not the winning of specific legal rights, but the change in attitude. It is a change in the social structure of society, so that you don't face when you graduate from university the same kind of shit I faced when I graduated. No one says to you, "We don't hire women here." They said that to me. That is achieved in one generation.

KR: I remember hearing you say a few years ago that things were going to be different now because we have a whole new generation of young women who've grown up believing they are equal. But society doesn't treat us equally yet. And women, who more often live in poverty, are being forced to bear the brunt of restructuring while we remain outside the centres of power. We need to prioritize our demands and develop some dynamic campaigns to see them through, to involve large numbers of women and revitalize feminist movement.

JR: True. And if we don't move forward, there is a good chance we will move backwards. One of the things that really drives me crazy is how little recognition the Canadian women's movement gets, even in Canada. Canadian feminists were ahead of American feminists from the beginning. *Chatelaine* magazine, under the editorship of Doris Anderson, was the first mass-circulation feminist magazine in the world. Doris told me a story about how Betty Friedan sent her manuscript for *The Feminine Mystique* to *Chatelaine* but they decided not to publish an excerpt from it because they had already written about all those issues. The 1970 Royal Commission on the Status of Women report stands as the most comprehensive government report on the status of women done in that historical period. Canada has the strongest equality guarantees in our charter, is one of the only countries that has removed abortion from the criminal code, has one of the most progressive rape laws, and was the first country to recognize gender persecution as a basis for refugee status. All of these achievements were fought for and won by feminists. And for all our problems, the organized women's movement in Canada is the most inclusive in the world. So we've done a lot of things right.

6

Beyond Inclusion

TRANSFORMING NAC

JR: The National Action Committee on the Status of Women, founded in 1972, is a federation of more than six hundred women's organizations from across Canada. The recent election of Joan Grant-Cummings as president of NAC really shows how far the women's movement has come in a brief period in transforming itself, and how far ahead of the rest of society we are. Within NAC, Joan's election was not the least bit controversial. She had been an integral part of a very popular leadership with former president Sunera Thobani and had done an excellent job as treasurer. She is a committed, knowledgeable activist. Joan's opponent, Catherine Laidlaw, was unknown to most NAC members. So there really wasn't much of a contest. Yet the media made the presidential election into a major race battle because Joan is Black and Catherine is white. Sunera Thobani had said that she would like to see a woman of colour replace her, but that remark was blown out of all proportion, and the suggestion was made by the media that Sunera was telling NAC members who to vote for and even that white women were guilted into voting for Joan.

KR: I think Sunera told the media that she wanted a woman of colour to follow her in the spirit of not wanting to be a token as NAC's first woman of colour president. It was said in the spirit of wanting to see the changes towards real inclusion stick.

The media often put the worst slant on things during the campaign. Not only were their accusations unfounded, they also insulted the delegates' intelligence and integrity. Joan was the better qualified candidate plain and simple. The press coverage diverted attention away from that. But the fact that Joan won 90 per cent of the vote and that a significant number of women of colour are serving on the NAC executive are to me signs that the changes within the organization are meaningful. I think both Sunera and Joan's elections represent the efforts of a decade's worth of work by women of colour to make anti-racism a feminist issue.

In the women's movement across the country in the late 1980s, women of colour were demanding more representation. They were saying that if the women's movement was really in favour of equality, it had to fight for all women, not just the privileged few. This was an incredibly intense struggle, especially in Toronto and Vancouver. Women of colour were debating whether to focus on building our own organizations like NOIVM, the National Organization of Immigrant and Visible Minority Women, or to participate in "mainstream" groups. Some women did both. The struggle for inclusion and representation became visible in NAC meetings around 1986.

JR: When I became president of NAC in 1990, there were two women of colour and three aboriginal women on an executive of twenty-five. That was the best representation we had ever had. There was no formal affirmative action policy in the organization then, even though the visible minority women's committee had proposed one, but women of colour had been organizing at NAC annual general meetings for several years. Salome Loucas, from Women Working with Immigrant Women in Toronto, was key in organizing the women of colour caucus, and she was elected onto the executive that year as a member at large. Prior to 1990, there were always one or two women of colour on the executive, but they were isolated.

Recently I had a discussion with Jon Leah Hopkins and Fleurette Osborne, two Black women who were on the NAC executive in the 1980s. Jon Leah said that it was tough in those days; NAC was full of "a lot of middle-class white women who wanted to be nice." She told me: "We all felt we weren't racist and wouldn't do racist things. But small things happened all the time. People cut me off when I was speaking. We were called the visible minority women's committee in those days. We were trying to organize women of colour in Quebec and Nova Scotia, but the executive just wouldn't provide money to organize outside Toronto. No one ever said 'no,' they just ignored us."

Here's an example I saw myself of how NAC ignored issues of racism. Resolutions to the AGM used to be organized in alphabetical order by subject, so "visible minority women" was near the end of the list. At the AGM in 1987, there were a significant number of women of colour in attendance for the first time. Their resolutions got dropped off the agenda, however, because we ran out of time and they were at the end of the list. That is how much attention NAC paid at that point to women of colour.

In my acceptance speech as president, I said my priority would be to see a transformation in NAC so that we would become more representative of women, including aboriginal women, women of colour, women with disabilities, and poor and working-class women. From the beginning this direction affected our work. In the summer of 1990, we did solidarity work with aboriginal women when the armed confrontation at Oka developed. That was the year after the defeat of the Meech Lake Accord. So another of NAC's priorities was to heal the split that had developed with Quebec women's groups. I proposed the idea of a cross-country tour with a francophone woman from Quebec, an aboriginal woman and a woman from somewhere else in Canada to discuss the constitutional issues. Salome Loucas argued that we should also have a woman of colour to bring in the issue of race. I disagreed, saying that the issue of racism was different from the issue of self-determination for Quebec and aboriginal peoples who are nations, and that it should be discussed in a different forum. Salome felt that no one was listening to her, and she walked out of the meeting. That was our first major confrontation on the issue of racism during my presidency. We decided to hold off on the idea of the tour until we could sort it all out. Well, we never had that tour. Salome joined the constitution committee, and we finally included the issues of racism and multiculturalism in our resolution on Quebec to the 1991 AGM.

At that AGM, NAC adopted an affirmative action resolution reserving five positions, one vice-president and four members at large, for women of colour, immigrant women of colour, women with disabilities and aboriginal women. Francophone women demanded inclusion in the affirmative action clause, and after much debate, we agreed to add another vice-president who would be designated francophone.

The affirmative action resolution did more than any other single action to transform NAC. The executive that year had a strong representation of women of colour and aboriginal women, about 30 per cent. We never did achieve the representation we wanted of women with disabilities, and NAC still hasn't, but the other groups have continued to be well represented. Sunera Thobani was elected as part of that executive.

In 1993, when Sunera was elected, the public attacks against her at first were vicious.

KR: I remember. That was the year I joined the NAC executive as a member at large. We had that ignorant Tory MP who wrongly said that Sunera was an illegal immigrant. That sparked demands for NAC's funding to be withdrawn, and the staff started getting a barrage of ugly, threatening phone calls and hate mail.

JR: Yes, it was shocking, but somewhat expected. What we *weren't* prepared for was the kind of transformation NAC itself would have to undergo, and frankly, I have been astonished by some of the problems that have cropped up.

KR: I'm not surprised at all. NAC's internal problems are linked to societal ones. It's not possible or useful to summarize here all the complexities of the internal difficulties the NAC executive has faced. But one of the more telling stories was an incident Sunera recalled when a white NAC executive member said in a meeting that the white women were there to "compensate for the lack of expertise of the women of colour," and none of the other board members challenged that statement.

Racism has prevented white women from working with women of colour as equals, and there are centuries of mistrust and exclusion to overcome. A lot of "progressive" white women might be willing or able to support a woman of colour whom they perceive as "disadvantaged," less well off than they are. But when it comes to actually having to share power, to accept leadership from that "marginalized" woman and place their trust in the woman of colour's vision and abilities, then I think many white women get scared. Because it means they have to abandon everything they were raised on their entire lives. White people usually only see people of colour taking orders, being in servile positions. A superiority complex in whites is learned and fostered from birth.

JR: Perhaps I shouldn't have been surprised. But if you're a feminist, and you understand the way patriarchy works, that notion of "natural" superiority among men, then you should be able to apply that to interrace politics, because it's the same dynamic.

KR: A lot of white women don't see it as the same dynamic because they're resistant to acknowledging that they've benefited from racism, that they can be and were oppressors, as slave mistresses, overseers, missionaries, supporters of colonization, and so on. White feminists might develop analyses and strategies for dealing with, say, workplace sexism. But when it comes to race, a lot of them get a mental block. When women of colour call white women on racist behaviour, a lot of the time white women respond by crying, by talking about their feelings of guilt or just by being defensive instead of trying to learn what went wrong and how to stop it. Acknowledging the kind of power and privilege you have as a white person means that you have to take responsibility for your actions. You can't just blame your behaviour on ignorance.

JR: Yes, I think part of it is a basic resistance to change. What Sunera has called "race solidarity" among white women: white women being very defensive and unwilling to look at anything they say or do as racism. But if there is one thing we have learned, it is that even once you remove barriers that exclude women of colour and aboriginal women, racism deforms and distorts relationships between people.

KR: Nobody will come right out and say, "I can't stand these people. I don't want them taking over *our* organization." But there's still a sense of proprietorship, like, "We were here first, we built this thing." There's no acknowledgement of the contributions of women of colour to feminist struggle or of the fact that we've been organizing separately all along. We have to raise the issues of exclusion all the time. But women of colour do not "own" racism as an issue. And often when we do raise it, white people do not listen to what we're actually saying. They don't want to hear it.

JR: I used to understand racism in a very analytical way: racism was a way to divide people. I was resistant to the notion that I was privileged as a white person. It wasn't till I was in NAC that I understood how it worked, how I would be accepted in a way that a woman of colour wouldn't. I started to see it when I started to talk about racism.

I spoke at a Canadian Labour Congress women's conference in 1991. Some Black women there did a silent protest, because there were the same small number of Black women at the conference as the year before and the year before that. June Veecock, the Ontario Federation of Labour's human rights director, made a passionate speech about "How come white women know how to fight for something when you want to fight, but when we ask you to fight for us, you're not there?" I could see that the white women weren't hearing what she was saying. So I wrote down word for word what she said, and then when I spoke I repeated it. I didn't say anything different, but when I said it the white women heard it. It was a dramatic moment for me, because the women there knew June and they didn't know me. I started to slowly become aware of what women of colour had been telling me about the insidious ways that racism works, what white-skin privilege means.

KR: When a white woman speaks up against racism, that opens the door for other whites to see that there is a way of being both white and anti-racist. Those two things together are rare, but not mutually exclusive. I say "rare" because most whites do not actively fight against racism. But until that happens, we as women of colour don't know who our allies are. We don't see that there is any support for our struggles. I think that most white women think, "Accept me as I am, I'm a good person, I'm involved in this social justice issue," but racism can be very subtle and deeply embedded.

JR: One thing that has become very clear to me is that as a white woman I could only go so far in leading the process of transforming NAC. It took the leadership of a woman of colour to really challenge the deep-seated racism embedded in the leadership structure and to convince women of colour across the country that NAC was truly their organization too. While I was president, we had debates, like about the affirmative action resolution, but there wasn't a fundamental change in the way the organization functioned. This is probably the hardest point to explain publicly.

KR: What the women of colour caucuses did and what you did, Judy, was to lay the ground for change. The idea of inclusion, the commitment to anti-racism, was there. But these are only the seeds. Unless they are allowed to grow and bear fruit, the work cannot be seen. These two latest presidencies and the increased participation of women of colour are a kind of incarnation of these principles. But the process of transformation does not stop there.

You can't expect to really challenge something as powerful as white domination without taking risks or making sacrifices. We shouldn't think that becoming an anti-racist organization just means having more women of colour members and executive. It has to be about the anti-racist perspective, the analysis, the alliances created and the ongoing campaigns NAC develops and carries forth. But right now we're so focussed on issues of representation.

Many are happy to "include" but ignore, so our inclusion alone can be superficial unless that presence makes a difference. I think NAC is under attack now not only because women of colour are in the leadership but because the organization is moving left of centre under that leadership. The further you are from the centre of power, the less likely you are to support the status quo. The more critical your perspective is likely to be. It's that analysis and the willingness to break with conformity that I think will serve the women's movement well, especially as the political and economic climate grows more right-wing and more women of all backgrounds find themselves marginalized.

JR: In 1992, NAC decided to lead the "No" campaign in the national referendum on the Charlottetown Accord. NAC opposed the accord because we thought it would weaken social programs and undermine equality rights. Even though the executive and the membership were opposed to the accord, it was very bold to campaign for a "No" vote because most of our allies were on the "Yes" side, and at the time the only force on the "No" side was the Reform Party. I am pretty sure that without the kind of representation we had on the executive from grassroots women, including women of colour and aboriginal women, NAC would never have made that decision. Middle-class professional women were much more wary of standing on the "No" side. There was tremendous pressure to "hold your nose and vote yes" to "save the country." The participation of immigrant women, some of whom had lived in repressive regimes, helped us to put NAC's position into perspective. Maybe the prime minister would accuse us of being traitors, but he wasn't going to put us in jail or torture us. And the aboriginal women brought a wisdom about process and a spiritual strength that helped us to have a calm and reasoned discussion. Sandra Delaronde, a Metis woman from Manitoba who was vice-president, told us that she was wearing her grandmother's scarf so that her grandmother and all the elders of her community would be with us and help us to make the wisest decision.

I think most of the racial conflict that arises is based on the different perceptions that women of colour and white women have of a particular issue, and on the difficulty of communicating across those differences. There is no question that white women and women of colour experience the world differently. We see issues through a different race lens, and these differences in perception and understanding have to be struggled through to come up with a position that everyone is satisfied with. The tension created by racism is inevitable in a mixed-race organization where people of colour play a major role, and it's through these struggles that an organization will be transformed.

The issue of hearing criticism as blame, as a personal attack, is one of the big problems we have. You do have to work through gender and race oppression at a personal level, as well as at a political level, in order to change anything. But when you take every political criticism personally, everything becomes about whether you're a good person or not. Women may struggle with their own guilt and do absolutely nothing to actually fight against racism in the world.

KR· Right White people should strive to decolonize their minds and fight against racism as a favour to themselves, not to anyone else. They should see it as a way to move beyond the lies they've been taught, and the guilt and fear. There's a lack of trust there because we don't see white people standing up and speaking out on issues of racial justice.

When Sunera Thobani became president, she and NAC were faced with a whole series of new challenges. For example, there is a perception that women of colour can't speak for a "mainstream" organization, can't really represent white women. I have this quote from an article in *Canadian Dimension* by a women's studies student named Heather O. Wood, who spoke honestly about initially feeling threatened by a woman of colour assuming the NAC presidency. She worried that "NAC would lose a lot of its credibility, power and influence because minority women are not valued as much or listened to as much as white women in our society. I didn't want a minority woman to be head of a powerful women's organization because she would bring a loss of status and esteem to the organization along with her." Of course NAC also *gained* a lot of credibility in the eyes of the women of colour organizations that have joined since Sunera's presidency. Because of Sunera's ability, NAC's membership and financial footing were strengthened. But what is also true is that when you focus on the issues of women who have been marginalized, you *get* marginalized by the mainstream.

JR: We can see it in so many ways. One example was the reaction of the media to NAC's demonstration against the Reform

Party at the 1994 AGM. The Reform Party refused to attend NAC's lobby, and so women marched into the parliament buildings to demand a meeting with Preston Manning. The security guards freaked out and things got out of hand. The media images were of angry women of colour tussling with security guards. Now, a similar thing happened when I was president. We marched on the parliament buildings in 1991 to demand a meeting with the government. The guards shut the doors in our faces, and women started to pound on the doors. In both cases the parliamentary press gallery reported the demonstrations in a very negative light. But in Sunera's case, they used the incident to justify the continued marginalization of NAC. In my case, it was soon forgotten.

KR: Because of this marginalization, I think the areas in which NAC was breaking ground during Sunera's presidency were overlooked. For example, the work on the social implications of new reproductive technologies and the new emphasis on building international solidarity in our movement and on ending poverty, which is probably the most important issue women face.

As much as some people want to talk about "colour blindness," this is a society where colour is seen as a primary decoder for who you are, what you do and what you are going to say. As NAC President, Sunera was out there talking about the federal budget, social policy reform and any number of different issues that affect all of us. Yet it was perceived by many whites that she only talked about racism or immigration.

JR: I've heard people say that, and I don't know what they are talking about. NAC focussed as much or more on immigration issues when I was president.

KR: I've noticed something similar in my own experience. I was in a situation where I spoke at a demo and press conferences as a NAC executive member about the Audrey Smith incident, which was the case of a Black woman who was strip-searched on a Toronto city street by the police. A little while later, I was at a Black Law Students Association of Canada conference about Black women's perspectives on the law. We entered into a discussion about the Audrey Smith case, and one woman complained that no one from NAC had said anything about it. She added, "How typical. The white mainstream organization doesn't care about us." Beverley Bain, a Black woman and former NAC executive director, said, "But wait a minute. We had an executive member speaking out about these issues." I think what happened was that, because I'm Black and I've spoken out on police brutality before, my Blackness was seen to the exclusion of my position as a representative of this "mainstream" organization. So while some whites were thinking a South Asian woman president made NAC too women-of-colour focussed, some people in the Black community were still thinking NAC was too white and didn't represent them. Not surprising, given NAC's very white, middle-class history. Another comment I heard indirectly came from a woman of colour who liked what I said at a rally but was afraid that white women might try to take advantage of me as a NAC executive member to cover for them on racism issues.

I think it's important to be supportive of positive change while remaining critical and vigilant. When we operate in mainstream organizations, then to some extent we're not allowed to introduce our own communities' concerns without seeming suspect. So women of colour taking on these kinds of positions have to deal with the issues of who they represent and how they bring forth different issues.

JR: I think a lot of white women face some pretty difficult dynamics too. For example, when Sunera first became president, some of the white women who were table officers (the executive of the executive) hung back and didn't volunteer to take on various positions. I believe the white women thought what they were doing was giving the women of colour room to take on responsibility. But the effect of their action was the opposite of what they intended. It left women of colour feeling that the white women were not supporting their leadership, and white women feeling more and more excluded. After a while, this polarization manifests itself in political or organizational differences along race lines. Unless someone is willing to step out of their racial group and name the dynamic that is happening, it will continue.

There are also examples of more overt racism in NAC that I have found shocking. At the AGM in 1995, I heard remarks like, "Women of colour are trying to take over NAC." And I'd respond, "Well, so does that mean women have taken over the Canadian Union of Public Employees, since CUPE now has a women president and secretary-treasurer?" The fact that feminists could be so unconscious of what they were saying blew my mind.

The dynamics within NAC have changed, and one of the things the challenge of building a multiracial leadership involves is a shift in power. People who can't commit to the new vision will fall away. We're going to lose good people, and I feel bad about that.

KR: I think it's up to feminists to encourage all women to get involved in the movement. But it's not our job to woo disaffected women who don't like a more left-leaning, anti-racist agenda back into the fold. When Joan Grant-Cummings was elected, she said, "I can't do this job alone. Everyone needs to be involved." But she said that NAC had not wooed her into serving. She joined because she has a commitment to social justice, just like the white women in NAC, who are still in the majority, have a commitment to social justice. That is the basis on which we unite and carry on.

JR: But the dynamics are very complicated on both sides. When white women see women they have respected for many years leaving NAC feeling hurt, it is hard for them to understand it, and it makes them feel perhaps there is no place in the organization for them any more either. And this we have to be careful about. One woman of colour on the executive told me she wasn't interested in working with anyone who was willing to work with a racist. But of course the woman she sees as a racist is not seen that way by the majority of white women she works with, so it gets pretty tough. I think there is too much of a tendency to write people off on both sides. Some white women can excuse walking away from the struggle because their feelings are hurt. And some women of colour, who don't have the luxury of walking away, tend to brand white women. I think your generation is in a better position to sort some of this out.

KR: I don't agree at all. Some might make careless comments, but in my experience women of colour working in mostly white organizations find it far from easy. I'm thinking of the women of colour I know who've walked away from jobs and organizations physically sick, exhausted from the racism they've had to fight while trying to do their work. We're called "difficult," "aggressive" and "hostile" when we do raise it, and polarization and isolation grow. So we consciously choose which issues to raise and which to ignore. We repress and internalize some of the hurt and anger.

As far as my generation goes, I think there is less excuse than ever to be ignorant today because of all the work our foremothers have done, and because of all the ground-breaking critical writing on race by women of colour. Definitely some young white women have sensitized themselves, but, to use one example, most of the newly prominent white women writing about contemporary feminism have chosen not to include the experiences of women of colour or a race analysis in their books.

JR: We need more white women and women of colour who have developed an analysis of racism. They have to be able to understand the dynamics and not be afraid to name them. There are not very many women around like that, particularly white women. So then, how do you do it?

KR: Well, for one thing, we need more tools for dealing with conflict, like giving and receiving criticism in a way that's useful, creating guidelines for dealing with grievances, stronger mediation skills. I think trying to build better representation right into the structure is helpful. Affirmative action steps are good. How can we champion something we don't practise? We have to start seeing more women of colour pervasively throughout the whole organization, on all of the committees, so that our realities can be integrated. It's a difficult transition to make. How do we build a support system for making meaningful change and not just parachute a single woman of colour onto each committee? How do we make it genuine so we're not just being tokenistic?

JR: Right. For example, even though there is leadership in NAC by women of colour, at the local level women of colour can still feel excluded from the organizing. I think what we have learned is that we have to make the structural changes and then pay a lot of attention to the dynamics that follow. One of the things we understood around women of colour being more integrated into NAC was that you had to have structures that rebalanced the power.

KR: I think what happens is that when a new group of women comes to occupy decision-making positions in a structure that is already there, the group who is then on the outside suddenly notices what the structure looks like and feels like and they become conscious of it in new ways.

JR: That's a good point. We have to really listen to each other. It is a lot tougher than I thought it would be. But there are big gains to be made if we can struggle through it. You know, the women's movement has always talked about feminist process, but I think through these struggles around racism, we are starting to actually define a different kind of process, where leadership really is representative of the membership and where power dynamics are equalized.

KR: For some women of colour, working in our own organizations remains the priority over joining mixed groups. Both are valid choices. I think we need to be rooted in our own communities first and build from there, build as wide and as strong a base of support as we can to sustain us emotionally and politically. We have to operate knowing what our agenda is, otherwise we'll only be responding to someone else's, and we should never make holding a position more important than using our position in the service of our vision. If we're losing our sense of self, if every day is a struggle of the wrong kind, then we might just have to leave and not worry about critics or the "chaos" that might ensue.

JR: I understand that. But it's not chaos, it's crisis. I'm persuaded now, after these past few years in NAC, that you can't make such a profound change without crisis. It requires people to struggle so much with their assumptions, and there is a lot of fear and anxiety. Change is always difficult, but when you are trying to create an anti-racist organization in the midst of a racist society, it's even tougher.

KR: I read somewhere that the Chinese character for "crisis" combines "danger" and "opportunity." I think the danger in not declaring racism a feminist issue and fighting to end it is that we kill feminism's vision of liberation for *all* women. But when we become anti-racist and embrace a multiracial leadership in the broadest sense, we help create a women's movement that makes democracy real.

7

If There's a Will, There's a Way

· ·

ENDING MALE VIOLENCE
AGAINST WOMEN

JR: Somewhere in the early seventies, an underground movement of survivors of violence or people who knew survivors
started to organize rape crisis centres and shelters. These early
shelters and rape crisis centres were very feminist, very radical.
Their goal was to empower women and give them a place to get
away from violent men. The workers who started these centres
saw their activity as an act of resistance. Vancouver Rape Relief
and the Toronto Rape Crisis Centre are examples of centres
started at that time. The issue of domestic violence did not interest the media quite as much as sexual assault, so work in that area
was more difficult. You may remember the story of Margaret
Mitchell, an NDP MP who in 1982 was laughed at by male MPs
when she raised the issue of battered women in the House of
Commons. Nevertheless, as a result of women's activism, domestic violence did become a growing concern in the public mind.

Today almost every community in Canada has a shelter, and major centres have rape crisis centres. That is a tremendous gain for women. Such centres remain the core of any strategy to end male violence against women.

KR: There's no question that shelters and crisis centres save women's lives, and they are an important gain. There were issues the shelter movement didn't address, though, namely the ways that women of colour and immigrant women of all racial backgrounds experience violence against them, and the difficulties they face in trying to get services that respond to their needs. This is especially true in a society that has racist, ethnocentric stereotypes about other "traditional" cultures. Just dealing with trying to support women facing violent men is a major piece of work, but when you add to that the need to deal with language barriers and the culture shock many immigrant women and refugee women face, not to mention their isolation, then you have to start confronting and challenging the system even more to get the resources these women need. Women of colour and immigrant women began to come together in the early eighties to talk about these issues and come up with solutions. The Shirley Samaroo House, established in 1987 in Toronto, was the only shelter in the country set up to respond to the specific needs of women of colour and immigrant women. The staff of most shelters was not racially and culturally diverse, and usually wasn't sensitized to deal with a lot of these issues. That's still true in many places.

JR: Despite their excellent work, centres today are finding it harder and harder to get funding. Because government won't deal with male violence against women as a major societal problem and mobilize all of society to eliminate it, as they did with drunk driving, for example, women's groups are constantly having to fight rear-guard actions. For the last ten years, rape crisis centres and shelters have had to fight in the courts to protect women from revictimization by defence attorneys, first through the rape law and now through the disclosure law. Statistics Canada's most recent report on the extent of violence against women is questioned in a way no other Stats Can study is questioned. Feminists are accused of blaming all men for violence against women, instead of men being asked why they don't do more to end this violence. There's even a raft of books and articles suggesting that most of the concern is exaggerated hysteria or the creation of twisted therapists, especially in the case of sexual assault and abuse within families.

KR: We have this paradox: many cases of violence against women, like that of Nicole Simpson, Leslie Mahaffy and Kristen French, the two young women murdered by Paul Bernardo, and Melanie Carpenter, a young woman who was kidnapped and killed in B.C., are sensationalized, but at the same time there is continued denial of the breadth of the problem of violence against women. We're left with the impression that violence against women is only the problem of a few antisocial men. This undermines the feminist analysis that violence against women is connected to women's inequality in society. There needs to be a broader understanding that women need more options, more social, political and especially economic power, to be able to leave violent situations. It's inequality that makes women vulnerable to violence.

JR: We've understood the relationship between male violence against women and the power inequalities between men and women for many years in the feminist community. But I think there is less understanding now in the public mind than there was five or six years ago. The emphasis has been more and more on law and order issues. Legal changes were necessary because women's lives were insufficiently valued. But in the current climate, this approach creates a situation where the power imbalance between men and women is disappearing as a public issue, and violence against women is being subsumed by violence in general.

You can see it in the differences in the way public discussion of the Paul Bernardo case, in 1995, has gone, compared to that of the Montreal massacre in 1989. After the women engineering students were shot in Montreal, violence against women moved to the front burner as a public issue. Feminists were able to counter the media's attempts to say that the gunman was just one crazy man. Women everywhere started talking about their experiences, and governments started to talk as if they were going to do something about it. In the case of Bernardo, who was convicted of the rape and murder of two women and pleaded guilty to the rape of many others, it was not violence against women that was being discussed, but violent crime. And it seemed to me that women themselves were almost afraid to talk about Bernardo as an extreme but nevertheless typical abuser of women.

This year, I even noticed a backlash against recognizing December 6 as a day to remember all female victims of violence. One woman called into a CBC Radio talk-back machine to say that she is very angry feminists are using December 6 to commemorate the women who were killed in Montreal. "What about the brave boys who were killed defending the women?" she asked. Of course, there were no men killed.

KR: In fact, one of the male students at the École Polytechnique in Montreal who was present when the women were shot later committed suicide, because he couldn't live with the fact that he hadn't done anything to stop the gunman. But I don't think the lack of feminist discussion of the Bernardo case was only because of the backlash. This case also raised disturbing issues for feminists, because Karla Homolka, who was married to Bernardo, actively participated in the torture and killing of the two young women and of her own sister. The prosecution passed Homolka off as Bernardo's victim, forced to do whatever her husband told her. I don't accept that at all. Yes, he beat her, but she seemed to willingly cooperate with the whole scenario. I think the fear for some feminists was that denouncing Homolka as a fraud would undermine the "battered woman syndrome" defence, which has been used successfully in cases where a woman who has been battered fought back, and somehow feed into the ridiculous myth sailing now that women are beating up just as much on men.

JR: Right. Despite police and Statistics Canada reports about the extent of male violence against women, the purveyors of backlash argue that women are just as violent as men in domestic situations but do less damage because they are not as strong. We can't counter these claims by refusing to admit that violent women do exist, however. What's the danger in admitting that? These women are products of the same patriarchal power relations that create violent men. It gets complicated, though. I was disturbed by a tendency in the media to blame Karla Homolka almost more than Paul Bernardo. She was his accomplice and she certainly has to be held accountable for that, but he bears the most responsibility for these crimes.

KR: There was also racism in this case, revealed by the way the police didn't follow up on tips and didn't suspect Bernardo and Homolka for a long time because they look like a nice, white, middle-class couple, which translates into "normal." Meanwhile, police routinely stop Black men on the street because they fit the description "Black male." The media presented it as shocking that this "golden-haired" couple, constantly shown in their wedding clothes, could be involved in something like that.

JR: Michele Landsberg, the *Toronto Star* columnist, has interviewed many of the women Paul Bernardo raped. She told me that the police had an excellent description of Bernardo before he moved to St. Catherines, before he had even married Karla Homolka, and that they had questioned him. In fact, they even had a DNA sample from him that sat on the shelf. But, as you say, because he was nice-looking, white and middle-class, they didn't pursue him. Michele said to me, "If that guy had been Black, they would have been on it in a flash. Racism helped kill those girls." And Lee Lakeman, a long-time member of Vancouver Rape Relief, told me that it is quite common for police to ignore information from rape victims.

I think all the media focus on the Bernardo case has really heightened fear among women, young women especially. A lot of backlash writers say that is what the feminist movement has done, too, by focussing so much on violence against women. Do you think it's true that we have helped to make young women too fearful?

KR: While I was at university in Montreal, the Polytechnique massacre happened in my first term. Five women were killed in one summer, all by their partners; two women in my neighbourhood were murdered; Concordia's Simone de Beauvoir Institute received bomb threats; I heard about a couple of rapes in frat houses; I went on a demo at a pedestrian underpass where several women had been attacked; each of my three roommates was flashed and followed by men, and one was almost attacked; and I had a hostile neighbour whom my landlord declared could not be violent because he was a student at McGill! The women's movement didn't make me conscious of violence; the news and my own experience did. The women's movement just gave me a framework to understand it.

But there's been a shift away from talking about the root causes of violence. It's part of this society's thirst to make everything quick and easy. Governments always prefer to set up a commission or fall back on law and order so that it looks like they're doing something. Politicians are cold on long-term solutions like building affordable housing for women and children running from violent men because these things cost money. But NAC's "99 Steps towards an End to Violence against Women" report showed that, since 1990, the government has spent over $20 million on *studies* on violence against women.

JR: And as Lee Lakeman, the author of that report, says, "With the millions in research that the government spent after the Montreal massacre, we have learned almost nothing that we didn't know already." We need to understand better why so many men feel they have permission and even support to beat women. During the national Women's March against Poverty, NAC renewed the demand for $50 million to fund rape crisis centres and shelters, and Finance Minister Paul Martin said the government had no money. This was just days after the feds had announced they would be giving $2 billion for training and employment services to the provinces. The message is clear. Ending violence against women is not a priority.

KR: With so much attention focussed on these high-profile, sensational cases, we get the impression that the problem is really individual men, and the solution is incarceration.

JR: That's true, but I think the women's movement has to take some responsibility here as well. A lot of us, myself included, ignored the issue of violence against women in the 1970s and 1980s. As socialist feminists, it just didn't fit into our ideological framework. We concentrated on issues like abortion, which were simple demands on the state, or issues like pay equity, which had to do with economic inequality. Liberal feminists were more focussed on constitutional change. So women resisting violence against women were isolated, and to a certain extent marginalized. For example, NAC did almost nothing on violence against women until the late 1980s, and this despite the fact that 40 per cent of its member groups were involved in anti-violence work. Also, a lot of the early debates in the women's movement did not arm us to fully understand solutions to violence against women. For example, the pornography debate degenerated into a bitter polarization that shed a lot of heat and not much light. And a lot of the theorists who write on violence against women, like Andrea Dworkin, have a radical feminist framework, that male oppression of women is the central problem of society. Dworkin talks about violence against women as male colonization of women's bodies. To me it's not a very useful framework, except in cases of actual sexual slavery, and it's easily misunderstood. But we do have to understand that male violence against women is about maintaining control and power over women, and that individual violence does have a societal role in keeping women in their place.

KR: I think there is a stream of socialist feminists of colour who did and do have a different understanding of the problem of violence against women. They developed an analysis that sexist violence is connected to patriarchy but that women experience that violence differently based on their race or class. And so their approach was to try to understand the forces of oppression in an integrated way. But these feminists also highlighted the contradictions of a state that punishes violent individuals but is itself violent, particularly towards people of colour and aboriginal people. In 1989, the Women's Coalition against Racism and Police Violence was formed in Toronto when a white male cop shot a young Black woman named Sophia Cook, paralyzing her. Women of colour also organized when Kay Poon, a Chinese woman, and Yvonne Taylor, a Black woman, were severely beaten by the police in Toronto.

JR: Debate about the relationship between institutional violence and male violence against women seems to emerge periodically in the women's movement. But an issue I would like to see a lot more debate about is the emphasis on justice issues. When violence against women started to get public recognition as a problem, it was quickly defined primarily as a justice issue. And professional women who could speak the language of politicians became the spokespeople for the movement. That began to change with the national justice consultations on violence against women begun under Kim Campbell in 1992 and continued with Allan Rock. Grassroots anti-violence workers now form majority of the group meeting every year with the justice minister. I think this process has really helped to shift some of the focus from a law-and-order approach to a more preventative one, at least at the national level.

But public attention to violence against women has concentrated more and more on the legal system, bringing in things like protocol for family violence, so that police are forced to lay a charge, and demanding strong sentencing. With the emphasis on victims' rights, the focus has shifted from the empowerment of women to the punishment of violent men. The parents of young women who have been killed by men are demanding longer

sentences and no parole, and even a return to the death penalty.
It's a difficult situation, because feminists certainly don't want to
contradict the parents of the victim.

KR: Many women working in rape crisis centres and shelters
have never trusted heavy legalistic intervention. Abused women
and their supporters are eloquent on the failures of the justice
system. But the law is often the last line of defence a woman has
to protect herself. Ruth Morris, a transformative justice activist,
reminded me that this society doesn't recognize or deal with
wrongs until it classifies them as crimes. It's taken us a long time
to get violence against women recognized as an injustice. Up until
1983 husbands who raped their wives were exempt from being
charged, to choose one example. So when the length of a jail term
becomes the only way to express the seriousness and ugliness of
a crime, you can see why women get angry when a guy gets five
years in jail for a property crime but only a couple of months for
rape. The state responds on legal issues because that doesn't
demand a fundamental change in its practice. We all know the
current system isn't feminist, doesn't give women a voice or real
protection. Often the men come out of jail more bitter.

JR: I agree that making the justice system recognize crimes
against women was essential, but we can't rely on it. I don't
believe sending men to jail does anything to eliminate violence
against women in the long term, and most women survivors of
violence never access the justice system at all. The justice system
doesn't work very well for any crime, but it is even more inade-
quate in dealing with violence against women.

KR: In the Black community and immigrant communities, the
problem of violence against women poses additional problems.

Inside the community it's still difficult to raise the issue, and it's even more difficult to seek outside help. A Black woman will find it difficult to call the police because our community has suffered a lot of police brutality. When recommendations are made for changes in the law, they can sometimes have an adverse impact on us. For example, on the one hand the police having to lay a charge in abusive situations means that the onus is taken off the woman, but fear that the police will lay a charge can be the very reason why the woman won't call for help in the first place.

JR: I think that is a problem for all women, although I agree it's more acute in communities that have reason to fear the police. I believe that mandatory charging has removed power from women. I know the arguments about women being intimidated by their batterers, but if we understand that being battered means being dominated and losing control, how does it help to give up all your control to the police and the courts? I think we have to find a way to give women victims of violence more control over the judicial process.

KR: Another problem is that other laws can work to make women more vulnerable: for example, the law that requires men to sponsor their wives in Canada for several years before the women can get landed status on their own. Abusive men often intimidate the women they've sponsored by threatening them with deportation. There are also the domestic workers laws, which make women dependent on living with their employers to stay in the country. Even in relation to shelters, we need multiple strategies, because for some women who live in small communities there aren't any shelters or services, and for others the idea of cutting themselves off from their community to go to a shelter or talk to a therapist may seem very strange.

JR: Yes. And women's groups have worked very hard to change these laws and to fight for more economic and social equality, but governments only respond to demands for stronger laws and stronger application of them. It seems to me that we have to redirect our energy.

KR: I think we won't make any progress unless violent men start to acknowledge the damage they do. Once you acknowledge as a woman that you've been a victim of violence, you have to do something about it: lay a charge, talk to somebody, go through therapy if that's what you need. But how can the perpetrator work through his action, confront it, acknowledge it, take responsibility for it? It seems like that is part of the problem too. Until the perpetrator feels shame and atones, he cannot be transformed. How does he say, "I did this and it was wrong," and mean it and make amends for it?

The idea of sentencing circles, where the victim and the perpetrator come together with family and community members to confront wrongdoing, is being tried in a few aboriginal communities. Some Native women have expressed concerns about the particular models that are being used and whether the way this process is being implemented works.

JR: You make a good point about perpetrators acknowledging wrong, but we have to be careful. A lot of batterers express tremendous regret after an assault and then do it again. I think the idea of taking responsibility and making amends makes sense, but we need to explore how it can work. I do believe we have to pay more attention to how to change men. After all, we are talking about male violence. I see this particularly in relation to young men, whom I think can change.

KR: There's no one easy answer. As a society we have to ask our-selves why we've created a male identity that rests so much on the domination of women and aggression of men. Men who know it's wrong have to speak out and stop collaborating with abuse. I think men need to learn how to understand and express their emotions better. But they won't change until the example is set in the whole society, by the people at the very top. As long as we continue to glorify and reward the "strong man with a gun," what incentive is there for men to embrace non-violence?

JR: One of the problems here is that a lot of groups look to repressive means of changing culture. They want to censor pornography or ban TV violence. But since these approaches don't deal with the root causes of violence, gender inequality and aggressive male socialization, they won't solve the problem. I think feminists should be putting our energy into supporting alternate cultural expressions that paint a different picture of gen-der roles and gender relations. I, for one, want to see more erotica, whether gay or straight, not less, but erotica rooted in egalitarian relationships.

And men have to deal with the reality that a lot of men are violent towards women. I heard Andrea Dworkin say in response to a question at a lecture: "It is interesting how I meet so many women who have been raped, but I never meet a rapist. I meet so many women who are battered, but never a batterer. I meet so many prostitutes, but never a man who uses a prostitute." Men have to challenge other men on this issue.

KR: The Million Man March on Washington, D.C., which brought together over a million African-American men in Octo-ber 1995, is the only time in my life that I have ever seen and heard men stand up and say publicly as a group: "We have wronged women. We have wronged each other. We must take responsibility and stop this. We must make amends, make reparations for the wrongs." Now whether those men are keeping up their pledge is another question.

I think we need a massive campaign to make male violence against women taboo in our society. A campaign that gets the entire work force, schools, communities, everyone to confront violence against women and work towards ending it. We start by breaking out of denial and encouraging collective responsibility. Too often men can rely on privacy and silent collaboration from the rest of us to carry on their abusive behaviour.

JR: I was outraged when the management of several companies of which businessman Earl Joudrie is either chairman of the board or a board member, including Canadian Tire, Abitibi Price, Unitel and Gulf Canada Resources Ltd., said the fact that Joudrie beat his wife was not an issue in terms of his continued service to them. If men who beat their wives were shunned by the community and found it hard to get jobs, I am sure this would have a greater effect than sending them to jail, which just reinforces their violent behaviour.

We should be debating the most effective methods to end male violence, not whether it exists or how widespread it is. Prevention is also key. I worry that with the right-wing shift, cutbacks will eliminate the anti-violence, pro-equality curriculum that is just beginning to be implemented in the schools. I think self-defence is important. Every young girl should take self-defence courses to get more physical and psychological self-confidence.

KR: We need to raise our daughters with high expectations for them to be independent, strong and intelligent, and as a society ensure that women have equal opportunities in everything.

JR: And we have to raise our sons to be non-violent and to treat women with respect.

8

Nation to Nation

• •

DEALING WITH QUEBEC

JR: The Quebec Referendum of October 1995 was probably the
most traumatic event for this country in a very long time. My
sense of what's happening now is that the two solitudes have
never been more divided. I was feeling before the referendum that
the Bloc Québécois being in Parliament helped people to understand a little better what the sovereignists were thinking. But the
shock of the referendum results, the almost-win of the sovereignists, was so great, both in the rest of Canada and in Quebec
among anglophones and allophones (those whose first language is
neither French nor English), that the impact has been a tremendous polarization. The debate is getting more and more radical, in
the worst sense of the word. It seems there's very little sympathy
now in the rest of the country for any kind of accommodation to
Quebec. A lot of people seem to have settled on the notion that the
federal government should take a hard line.

KR: Right. We're hearing more angry, frustrated anglophone voices seriously saying, "If Quebec wants to leave, let them go. Just take away their passports, take away their privileges and let's be done with it."

JR: I think that the unity rally held in Montreal a few days before the referendum vote, where people came from all over the country to say "Please stay," was like the last-ditch effort of a neglectful husband who reacts to his wife's announcement that she's leaving him by bringing home flowers and saying, "I'm going to be good and I'm going to come home every night and take care of the kids." Then, if his wife still leaves, he's a thousand times more angry.

KR: Only in this case, the rest of Canada wasn't even promising a change in behaviour. The message stopped at, "Don't go. We love you."

JR: I think a lot of people genuinely went to express their desire for Quebec to stay in Canada. But there was no understanding of the issues. It was total emotionalism. And the result is that people feel spurned.

KR: I understand people's sense of wanting to do something to keep the country together. But I think that as long as we don't know or understand how we got into this mess in the first place, as long as we don't have the details of the debate, gestures towards unity will be just that, gestures, and not solutions. The media did a poor job of giving people information. Nobody really knows what "partnership" with Quebec means or what "sovereignty with association" is, but so many are solidly against it. There was also a serious failure of leadership from the government and politicians. Many francophone Quebecers did not see the rally as a gesture of solidarity but one of arrogance: anglophones coming in at the last minute to tell them how to exercise their vote and not respecting the right of the people of Quebec to decide their own fate. During the whole time, no one really addressed the long-standing grievances that Quebec has had over a couple hundred years or the question of sovereignty for First Nations people, who have been here for thousands of years.

JR: A failure of political leadership has been a constant feature of the constitutional saga in Canada. At the constitutional conferences that were organized by the Tories in 1991, in a desperate attempt to get some public support for constitutional change after Meech Lake and in the lead-up to Charlottetown, NAC and other like-minded groups actually persuaded the majority of participants to support asymmetrical federalism or special status for Quebec—the notion that Quebec would have powers different from the other provinces—as a way of solving the national unity problem. But none of the politicians had the guts to stand up and argue for it.

There are a number of problems. One is the notion of ten equal provinces, which is related to right-wing notions of equality.

KR: The notion that equality means treating everybody exactly the same.

JR: Yes. It's related to the anti-aboriginal backlash in B.C., where Liberal leader Gordon Campbell says, "One law for all British Columbians." And we know what he really means is no treaty rights for Native peoples. This notion of ten equal provinces doesn't just come from the Right; former Newfoundland premier Clyde Wells was the most eloquent spokesperson for it. But it has been so reinforced now that people assume if Quebec has more powers, then the people of Quebec will have more rights. So there is just no arguing any more for a different kind of status for Quebec.

The second problem is that the definition of self-determination is so confused. We hear these arguments that a vote to separate has to be more than 50 per cent plus one, or that if Quebec has the right to vote to separate, then so does the west end of Montreal. And I blame the politicians for this confusion a lot more than I blame the media. The federalist politicians have totally misled us on this issue. They've never really said what they think. Then you have the Quebec federalists, who act like spoiled children, saying, "Give us more or there'll be separation," which really irritates people. And then you had the stupidity of the Charlottetown Accord, where they wanted to give Quebec more seats in the House of Commons. Quebec didn't even *want* more seats in the House of Commons. So I think there's been poor leadership, and now we have not only polarization between Canada and Quebec but incredible polarization inside Quebec.

KR: You talked about the two solitudes coming to the fore. Well, there really are many solitudes. There are different aboriginal nations in Quebec, the Inuit, the Huron, the Innu, the Mohawk and the Cree being some of them, who were largely ignored in this debate. I've heard some people make bizarre statements about equality and even distinctiveness, saying things like, "Well, Newfoundland is distinct." But because of their history on Turtle Island, as Native people call North America, aboriginal peoples cannot be treated as just another ethnic group. Long before European settlers came, Native peoples governed themselves with their own institutions, their own languages and forms of worship. The French too have a separate language, culture and set of institutions, and they governed themselves before the English came. But we have to look at their positions in a different way. We have to come to grips with the way Canada's constitution was shaped from the time of the British North America Act to the constitution's repatriation in 1982. When you don't have all the major players at the table, then what you get is what we have now, which is basically a constitution that sets up English people as dominant over everyone else.

JR: In Charlottetown, representatives of these groups were all sitting at the table, and they came up with a proposal that was rejected by everyone—aboriginal people, Quebec and the rest of Canada. So while I agree that having all parties at the table is important, it doesn't necessary produce results. A major barrier now is the fact that the premiers are the gatekeepers to the constitution because of the amending formula in the 1982 constitution. That makes constitutional change difficult, and the new regional veto adopted by Parliament makes it almost impossible. I think a more popular process is necessary, one that includes all three national communities, but not only leaders.

KR: Not everyone was there. The Native Women's Association wasn't there.

JR: And the sovereignists weren't there. But the government of Quebec was there, and the elected aboriginal leadership was there.

KR: I'm not just talking about Charlottetown. Right from the start is what I'm talking about. Right from the start, First Nations and European settlers had agreements, for example the Two Row Wampum treaty, which basically said that Native peoples and European peoples were to live on Turtle Island as equals, with respect and in harmony, but independently. They were to go their separate ways, co-operating where necessary but not interfering in each other's affairs.

Some of the problems around sovereignty started because the European settlers never honoured this agreement, or most of the others they entered into. If you look at the Royal Proclamation of 1763, you see that even when the English formally state that First Nations have not ceded Turtle Island or sold it to them, they continue talking about this place as "our dominions and territories" and about Native nations living under their "protection." So the Two Row Wampum principles got totally annihilated and replaced with Anglo domination over everybody.

JR: But the average person in Canada would not agree with that analysis.

KR: They might not, but that is the crux of the problem. This lack of recognition and reparation is what I see the debate centred around, though this is not said publicly very often. People don't understand the Québécois to be a colonized people because they came as colonizers. They did come here as settlers, but they were also oppressed by the English. There are many examples of this in Canadian history. When French-speaking people tried to assert their rights, they were deported to Louisiana and even Australia, and some were hanged. When they tried to stand up and say, "We want to be our own nation, we want to have some kind of self-determination," they were crushed; for example, during the Papineau and Riel rebellions. Meanwhile, aboriginal people were being wiped out or pushed onto reserves. English Canada does not want to deal with that history. They don't want to address the question of fundamental equal rights that have been denied.

JR: But it's not just a problem with English Canada. The aboriginal leadership, for example, have not argued that way either. The aboriginal people of Quebec have not argued, "Well, the problem is Anglo domination over everyone." They say the problem is if Quebec separates, they want to stay in Canada. So the position you're arguing now, not even the sovereignists argue that any more. They say they don't see themselves as oppressed any more, they just want their own country.

KR: It's not correct to say that no one argues what I'm saying. The sovereignists and the First Nations people may not use the same words I'm using now, but if you look at history and at more contemporary events, it is clear that the source of strife in this country is that there is an imbalance of power between the different peoples or nations that exist within Canada's borders. Every one of the nations that exist within these borders has been colonized by the English, and today we all live under a British constitutional monarchy. It would be nice if we could have a deeper analysis of what the real message of the Cree referendum was. The Cree voted 96 per cent against Quebec independence in their own referendum, held before the Quebec referendum. Were the Cree saying that they don't feel English colonialism is a problem, or that English colonizers are preferable to French ones? I don't think they're saying either of those things. The message I got from what I've heard Cree Grand Chief Matthew Coon Come say is that Native people's rights cannot be overlooked, that the Cree cannot be taken for granted. We also have to remember that the Cree form one of about ten Native nations in Quebec. Kahn-Tineta Horn, a Mohawk activist, has said that aboriginal people want to negotiate nation to nation.

On the Québécois side, former premier Jacques Parizeau once

said, "We were a French colony, then we became an English colony and now we want to be a sovereign nation." You're right that the Parti Québécois does not say, "We are an oppressed people." They can't say that because they are trying to negotiate with Canada as equals. But they have not forgotten their history as a people who were defeated by the English. The preamble of the accord that Jacques Parizeau, Lucien Bouchard and Action Democratique head Mario Dumont signed, the document that was the basis for the referendum vote, talks about the battle of the Plains of Abraham in 1759, where the English defeated the French. At the sovereignists' rally on referendum night, Dumont talked about Jean Chrétien's betrayal of the people of Quebec when he signed the constitution in 1982 without the consent of the Québécois people. Dumont ridiculed Chrétien for bowing down in front of the Queen of England. So it is not correct to think that history is not the major issue here. The problem of Canada *is* the problem of history.

JR: But just try and persuade progressive people, people on the Left, that we should support Quebec's right to self-determination on that basis. I have tried arguing the history, but people say that was then and this is now. As well as having the general backlash, there is also a backlash on the Left. Whereas in the eighties most people on the Left would have been sympathetic to the sovereignist movement, today they are not, for a number of reasons. One is that they see Bouchard and Parizeau as leaders who are not exactly progressive, even though they sometimes talk that way. Secondly, the aboriginal position in Quebec has been quite hostile to the sovereignty movement. Third, Quebec helped to bring in free trade and has been supportive of it. Fourth and not least is the fact that all or almost all of the cultural communities in Quebec, the racial minority groups, support federalism. So it's very difficult to argue anywhere in Canada today for accommodation with Quebec.

KR: After excluding and dissing them, the PQ can't expect the support of people in the "cultural communities," as they are called in Quebec. (I find all these different terms to name groups really problematic, but use them for lack of better words.) I think it is up to progressive people in the rest of Canada and Quebec to try to change the tenor of the debate to one of recognition, respect and reconciliation. As for the other issues you raised—I think people associate free trade more with the Tories, and don't really see sovereignists as playing a special role in that. Also, there is too much fixation on Parizeau and Bouchard as personalities. They are today's major spokespersons of the sovereignty movement, but tomorrow it could be someone else, so whether we like Parizeau and Bouchard or not is not the issue. They represent the aspirations of at least a few million people. As progressive people, we should never abandon the idea that a people have a democratic right to decide their own fate.

JR: Quebec wants first and foremost recognition as a people, a nation, and then they want more control over their own affairs. I think that the people of Quebec have the right to decide if they don't want to be a part of Canada. I believe that fundamentally, and I'll defend that. But I feel that out-and-out sovereignty will create both in Canada and in Quebec very negative conditions for progressive social change. If we could come up with a serious proposal for autonomy for Quebec, we wouldn't have to have the rupture. I think the reason that doesn't happen is that all the federalists in Ottawa, particularly the Quebec federalists, have a vested interest in maintaining the status quo, because without it they lose their power. That is the reason for the impasse. That, and the power-grabbing of the provincial premiers.

KR: I believe the reason we don't deal with the real issues is that it would mean the powerful would have to make reparations for wrongdoing.

JR: I don't think this question is so easy to solve. I think NAC has the right position, which is that Canada is composed of three nations or national communities, each of which is multicultural and multiracial: the aboriginal nations, Quebec and the rest of Canada. And that each nation has the right to self-determination—that is, to decide what form that nation should take. And that there should be negotiations among the nations to determine what their relationship will be. It's a position that would maintain a strong central government for the rest of Canada, and one that would recognize the inherent rights of aboriginal people both in Quebec and in Canada.

KR: This whole discussion of partition we're hearing now is so one-sided. What if aboriginal nations across this country were to say, "We want to separate from the rest of Canada," which would be well within their right? How much of the rest of "Canada" would be left over?

JR: Exactly. It's very dangerous to have a different discussion about what happens to aboriginal people in Quebec. It's hypocritical. The federalists can say, "Oh, if Quebec separates, the Cree have the right to separate from Quebec." But then do the Haida have the right to separate from British Columbia? Is the Indian Affairs minister going to support that?

The more polarized the debate gets, the more likely it is that partnership becomes impossible and separation happens. That worries me a lot. I think there is even the potential for violence, especially with this talk of partitioning Montreal.

KR: I'm dismayed by the talk of violence but also by some of the analysis about the cultural communities. After the referendum, some so-called "ethnic" papers were saying, "We won the day. We saved Canada," because the cultural communities voted overwhelmingly in favour of federalism. Some said that this was the triumph of Trudeau's vision of multiculturalism. But I think that line of argument is misleading. After all, you could just as easily say that simply not enough Québécois of French descent voted for separation. They are still in the majority in Quebec. That's partly why Parizeau was so wrong to blame the sovereignists' defeat on "money and the ethnic vote," as he so infamously put it. Allophones and more recent immigrants shouldn't be singled out for any special praise *or* blame. I also find it hypocritical when people get upset about Parizeau's racism but are silent when politicians in the rest of Canada say racist things about immigrants. In both cases the racism is meant to delegitimize the presence and full participation of the targeted group.

JR: We rarely saw anyone from the racial minority communities in Montreal in the media during the referendum debate.

KR: True. I was thinking about the impact of official multiculturalism in all this, too. Someone like me could almost have been Pierre Trudeau's dream child. Here I am a first-generation Canadian, who though born and raised in Toronto went to French immersion school, learned to speak the language and learned about French culture and Quebec. I went to live in Quebec and had mobility in that sense as a bilingual Canadian. And at one point, I thought Trudeau was a really progressive guy who promoted values of cultural harmony. But I say "almost" because I now have a greater awareness of Canadian history. And I see now how the idea and policies of multiculturalism that Trudeau developed have been misused to thwart Québécois nationalist feelings and buy votes for the Liberal Party. The federal government has traditionally dealt with the Quebec nationalist question by containment or by adopting a violent, hard-line approach, like when they invoked the War Measures Act in 1970.

JR: Trudeau's vision of the country was two languages, many cultures. I've always defended bilingualism even though I knew it was a mythology. Canada is not a bilingual country. The only places that I consider bilingual in Canada are Ottawa and Montreal. Canada is bilingual only in the sense that you can access the courts and the government in two languages. The multiculturalism program, in its initial stages anyway, was a form of patronage from the Liberal Party to get votes from the ethnic communities. Since then it's become better, because it has funded some anti-racist initiatives. I've always defended bilingualism and multiculturalism against the yahoos who oppose these things because they don't want to see French on cereal boxes or non-white immigration. But when I hear Andrew Cardozo, an Ottawa anti-racist activist, argue that official multiculturalism has worked because the ethnic minorities in Quebec all voted yes for Canada, I don't agree. I think there is such strong "No" support among allophones for a couple of reasons. Until very recently, when Bill 101 went into effect, immigrants moving to Quebec wanted to learn English because it was easier to get a job if you spoke English than if you spoke French. Speaking English was the way to get ahead. The second thing is the underbelly of ethnic nationalism in the Quebec sovereignist movement. While I agree with you that there are other politicians in the rest of Canada who have said racist things, I have never heard any of them say anything as awful, as racist as what Parizeau said on referendum night. It wasn't just the "money and the ethnics" line that bothered me. It was when he said, *"We know who we are."* At that moment he was talking about Quebec as the francophones of Quebec, the *pure laine* francophones.

Despite the fact that Quebec has strong legal protection for minorities in its charter, and that most sovereignists recoiled at Parizeau's remarks, every nationalist movement risks declining into chauvinism, and that is scary. The Quebec nationalist movement has to become actively anti-racist if they want to convince anybody who is in a racial minority in Quebec to support them.

KR: I think there are other reasons why both francophones and the allophone/cultural community groups are feeling shaky. And that is what is happening in the world at large, all the rapid changes brought by globalization, technology, loss of jobs. People are worried about their futures. The response of a lot of allophones is to stick with the safer bet, which to them is Canada, the country to which they or their parents emigrated. Whereas for francophone sovereignists, intent on preserving their culture in a sea of English, the solution lies in gaining power and control over their destiny.

JR: But if people are looking for stability, one would think that support for sovereignty would be declining instead of increasing. I think one thing fuelling support for sovereignty within Quebec is that the federal politicians have done all the wrong things to respond to Quebec. Federal politicians did try to convince the rest of the country to support the "distinct society" clause in the

Meech Lake Accord. But as opposition to the idea grew, the federal politicians watered down their arguments. Instead of clearly explaining the need to recognize Quebec's identity and to accord Quebec the powers it needs to protect that identity, today they argue, "Well, let's put 'distinct society' in the constitution because we promised Quebec we would and it doesn't really mean anything anyway." No one is going to be fooled by that.

KR: Just a "distinct society" clause now will probably be seen as too little, too late.

JR: Another way politicians try to respond to the sovereignty movement is the rush to decentralization. The other premiers say, "We'll give more power to *all* the provinces, and that will satisfy Quebec." They tried it with the Meech Lake Accord and even more so in Charlottetown. A lot of Canadians rejected both accords because of the decentralization proposals. But now the Liberals have done it anyway, through the budget and without constitutional change. Ironically, as a result of this decentralization and the cutbacks to social programs, there's less and less of a reason for Quebec to stay in Canada.

KR: During the referendum the Parti Québécois slogan was "*Oui et ça devient possible*"—"Yes, and it becomes possible." The sovereignists were saying yes to a vision. All the details of that vision are still largely undefined, but in the rest of Canada politicians are so busy chopping and burning that the question becomes, what do we really have to offer Quebec? All of these threats are made about financial loss and about Quebec being excommunicated from the entire world economy. But all the feds offer us is an agenda of cutbacks, restraint and downward mobility.

JR: Absolutely. I also think all this hard-line federalist sloga-neering is very frightening. After the first election in Czechoslovakia in June 1990, only about 6 per cent of the population, 5 per cent of Czechs and 8 per cent of Slovaks, wanted division. And then some politicians started whipping up nationalism, and by July 1992 you had 46 per cent of Czechs and 61 per cent of Slovaks favouring a split, and over 80 per cent of both groups believing that separation was inevitable. So they separated, and now people say, "What did we do that for?" Every time I say anything positive about the Bloc Québécois or the PQ or anything about accommodating Quebec on *Face Off,* you should see the letters I get! They call me a traitor, a bad Canadian. I don't get mail like that on any other topic. Ethnic nationalism is being reinforced in this country on both sides. The civility gets ripped away.

KR: And the discussion gets so backward, with English Canada and the Québécois fighting verbally over who will get to "keep the Natives." From the suggestions of the partition movement to the idea of giving every region of Canada a veto to threats, there is really no sensible strategy at all.

JR: Well, it's a strategy to increase polarization. But I don't think it's going to scare people in Quebec to vote "No." I think it will have the opposite effect. In the face of all this polarization, I think it's crucial to maintain the links in our social movements. One of the things we've done in the women's movement, with the exception of the breech with Quebec feminists around Meech Lake, is that we have managed to maintain common activities around fighting cutbacks, preserving social programs, working to stop violence against women. I think that's true in the labour movement as well. Certainly in the case of the Canadian Labour Congress, with which the Quebec Federation of Labour has a kind of sovereignty association arrangement. It's very important that we maintain those links, because if there is another referendum or election, we will need sane voices and the ability to dialogue with the people of Quebec at a grassroots level, and respecting each other is going to be critical. Actually, I think the social movements have a lot to teach the country about how to deal with Quebec.

KR: The "just say yes and we can have it all" referendum message obviously had to be taken with a grain of salt considering global economic pressures. Nevertheless, they were words of hope to many. But now the PQ government is dealing with the province's budget, with the debt and deficit issue there, promising that its cutbacks will be more "humane." Women in Quebec have just had another mass anti-poverty march.

One thing we need to understand in the rest of Canada is that there are different strains within the sovereignty movement. There is the racist ethnic nationalist strain, but there is also a current of people who have tried hard over many years to come up with a social justice vision of Quebec. Groups like Solidarité Populaire Québec, a coalition of community and labour organizations who worked together to create a "Charter for a People's Quebec," which has a progressive, anti-racist approach to Quebec sovereignty that also recognizes First Nations' right to self-determination. These voices are never heard in the mainstream media, but they should be, because that would give ordinary people a chance to talk about what really matters to us—creating a society that we all want to live in, with governments that actually respond to our needs.

JR: I think it is harder for alternate visions either in Quebec or in the rest of Canada to be heard on this issue than on any other because the stakes are so high. So the challenge becomes, how can

we break through that silence? Coming up with a common proposal between people in Quebec and people in the rest of the country for a partnership might be one way to get attention, because
it would be different, especially if both sovereignists and federalists were involved. It would show there can be respectful
solidarity.

KR: It's hard to decide all these questions by just marking "Yes"
or "No" on a ballot. People need to participate more in defining
the kind of nation we want to live in. The debate has to go beyond
Ottawa.

JR: In popular assemblies, I think people might be able to come
up with solutions. This approach was tried in the constitutional
conferences before Charlottetown and also in the CBC TV special
"72 Hours to Remake Canada." One possible solution might be
that the Quebec government gets many more powers but gives up
representation at the federal level as a trade-off. Or that we have
a two-nation federation similar to that in Belgium. There would
be a parliament for Canada and a parliament for Quebec and a
bicameral upper house that could debate and decide issues of common concern. Quebec would demand equal seats in that upper
house, but that would be a matter for negotiation. Of course, for
any of these proposals to be successful, the rest of Canada would
have to define itself and decide what kind of organization among
the provinces it would want to have. Too much of our national
debate has centred on how to keep Quebec in confederation and
not enough on what kind of country we want. I also believe that
if we could discuss some of these alternatives, it might help to
soften the blow if Quebec does proceed to another referendum and
obtains a "Yes" vote for sovereignty. By then it would be clear to
everyone that a partnership is possible.

KR: Yes. But we need to break out of the colonial language of "two founding nations," which denies the reality and the history of the First Nations of this land. We need to listen to and consider the options First Nations bring to the table for a new partnership. They have been the architects of many successful formations of government, like the Iroquois confederacy. But it'll be essential that Native women, who as clan mothers played such key roles as decision-makers throughout history, be integrated into the process on their own terms.

This is a complex and challenging task, but the other option is to accept a "unity" glued together by threats of financial loss or violence. In this day and age, when the notion of a "nation" is rapidly and dramatically transforming, we *can* come up with new and better ways of relating.

9

The Feminization of Power

. . . .

LEADERSHIP AND PARTY POLITICS

KR: One thing human rights movements have done is transform our notions of what leadership means. What makes you a leader is not that you're elected to some position but that you are committed to making people's lives better. So, to my mind, leaders are Black women like Harriet Tubman, who freed three hundred enslaved people and led them to Canada, or Rosa Parks, who refused to give up her seat to a white man on a city bus in the southern U.S. in 1955. She was arrested, but without saying a word, Rosa Parks inspired oppressed Black people to rise up. That simple, dignified act of defiance really stirred people.

What's amazing about our progressive movements is that without guns or lots of money we've made so many radical changes to society, making it more just. That's what good leadership does. You have to love and care about people on the ground. You have to be wherever they are, singling out the issues that are important to them with intelligence and a sense of history. You have to have courage, be a risk-taker and make some sacrifices. You have to speak truth to power.

But leadership means more than taking a stand on issues. It's also about how you pursue the vision for equality. I think the feminist movement has been at the forefront in trying to change group practices so that decisions and directions are not imposed and everyone feels like she has a vital role to play in making the movement successful. Being open to diversity, being inclusive, building consensus: they all sound like catch phrases, but the ideas behind them are revolutionary. They're a rejection of the hierarchical way we've been trained to respect and obey. For oppressed people, the way we gain power is by sharing power. None of us is really safe unless our group is safe.

So trying to achieve consensus and working on a collective model makes sense. But just because there are no stated leaders in a group doesn't mean that some people don't make their influence felt more than others. I still sometimes see the same jealousies and undermining going on in progressive groups. Some in the women's movement see strong leadership in individual women as threatening or as "male parroting." But people have different talents and strengths, and the thing to do is not to suppress these so that everyone can be "equal" but to bring out the different skills each person has and recognize and appreciate them.

People themselves are the ones who make real change. But inspirational leaders can really open your eyes and tell you something that you know already, in a way that makes you want to move from *knowing* it to *doing* something about it.

JR: The biggest challenge of leadership in progressive movements is how to lead in a bottom-up rather than a top-down way. I don't think that collectives without stated leaders are a good alternative. Our experience in the women's movement shows that there are always leaders who emerge. If we pretend we don't have leaders, then there is either a terrible lack of accountability on the part of those leaders or a process of trashing anyone who takes on leadership responsibility. I also think individual leaders are important on a mass scale. People relate to leaders as much as they do to issues. So I think we need leaders in progressive movements, but they must be leaders who share power, not leaders who monopolize power.

The big issue is accountability. A leader has to be truly representative of the group or movement she is leading. Not polling the membership every time you make a move, but really listening to your members and supporters.

I'll give you an example. During the constitutional debate leading up to the Charlottetown Accord, the constitution committee in NAC decided that we should call for gender parity in the elected Senate. This was not a priority that the NAC executive or membership had voted on. It was a tactical decision. The West was demanding a Triple E Senate, and it made sense in the context of our politics that if there was to be equality for the provinces, we should demand equality for women too. But we also felt that it was the one place we could win something leading up to Charlottetown, especially at the Charlottetown conference itself, and that by winning we would get more credibility on the other issues, like the Canada clause, charter protection for Native women and protection of social programs.

I took a lot of shit for that decision. The public attacks against NAC were mainly for other reasons, but internally the biggest, most controversial thing we did on Charlottetown was to push for gender parity in the Senate. Not because women didn't agree with it in principle, but because they thought we'd end up with more conservative women in the Senate. And they didn't see that as a progressive step. They also thought that too much energy was being focussed on this debate and not enough on the other issues. So this is a good example of where you might have to move before everybody's willing to support something, but then you've got to come back and explain why you did it.

In fact, this tactic worked exactly how we thought it would work. Bob Rae, Mike Harcourt and Donald Cameron, then the premiers for Ontario, B.C. and Nova Scotia, said they would organize the election of senators in their province along the lines of gender parity. Some other premiers were also considering it. So suddenly NAC was seen by the media as a player, and they started paying more attention to other things we were saying.

KR: The idea of moving ahead but explaining what you're doing is really key. While I was a student at McGill University, I got together with two South Asian women to form a group of women of colour called SHAKTI. There was a lot of resistance to it. Even before we had our first meeting, a white woman wrote an article about how wrong what we were doing was. But I was surprised when two women of colour came to our meeting and opposed us too. I spent a lot of time explaining why SHAKTI had a right to exist. One South Asian woman in particular kept coming back to the meetings and insisting that whites should be included. Finally someone talked to this woman separately. We discovered that she had grown up surrounded by white people, and she had always tried to gain their approval. She came to that realization for the first time through the discussion, and she later on became a big SHAKTI supporter.

JR: But sometimes moving ahead doesn't work. I'll use the example of the Canadian Panel on Violence against Women, established by the Mulroney government in 1991. Despite the fact that the panel was not sufficiently representative of women of colour and its mandate was unclear, I thought NAC had to support it. The chair of NAC's anti-violence committee was against NAC's participation on the advisory council of the panel, and so were many members of the executive. But I felt that we would lose too much credibility by refusing to co-operate. I won the vote on the executive, but I was wrong, and when NAC finally had to withdraw our support many months later, it was much more destructive than it would have been earlier. Here I was too influenced by my perception of how the media would react and not enough by what people on the ground were telling me. I admitted that I had been wrong, but NAC and the women's movement paid a price for that mistake. A lot of our critics think the mistake was to withdraw from the advisory council and boycott the panel. But our real mistake was to participate in the first place. That panel had zero credibility with women on the ground in the anti-violence movement or with women of colour groups, and those groups were our members. I think what happens to a lot of people in leadership positions is that they become too full of themselves and too sure of themselves and don't listen any more and think that they know better.

KR: There's a need for some genuine humility. You don't want stardom to override the message. A good leader also encourages good leadership in other people. She might take a forefront kind of role, but she's not afraid to delegate or share power. Because that's another thing that's dangerous. People in a community or movement can continually look to a particular leader to speak out on every single issue. That is a trap that weakens the group. So one of the things you have to do as a leader is to make sure other people are feeling confident in speaking out and developing agendas and strategies for themselves.

JR: I actually think stardom is important. When you're on the Left, being a star usually means that people are really connecting to what you are saying and doing. But given the cult of personality in our culture, it is important to keep stardom in perspective. Rather than playing down individuals and avoiding the star syndrome, I think what makes more sense is rotating leadership roles. And I think knowing when to step aside is important for a leader. So is developing new people, and recognizing and encouraging leadership in young people. When I'm looking for leadership in younger women in particular, I look for someone who is really dedicated, committed, articulate, willing to work hard. All those things. There are people around like that. But we're not encouraged to develop leadership in ourselves, and we don't have good training grounds, particularly on the Left. The good thing about far Left organizations is that they encourage the development of leadership. Their notion that they're developing the cadre to lead a revolution in the future is absurdly elitist, but it means that they train people in leadership skills. So when I was in the Revolutionary Marxist Group as a young person, I was trained in speaking and writing skills. I was really thinking and strategizing, and that has served me well all my life. We don't do that enough. They certainly don't do it in political parties, except by training organizers and candidates. Young people often show leadership by opposing the adult leaders. Understanding that and supporting it is very, very important. I think one of the reasons leadership is so weak right now on the Left is that there's no mainstream progressive group that's actually fostered and developed it in the last twenty years.

The women's movement has done the best job, because we actually have had a change in leadership. When you look at the women's movement in the United States, you've got the same leaders in all those organizations who have been there for twenty years. In Canada that's not true. A new generation of women are now leading the women's movement, and that's very positive.

KR: I think most of what I've learned about thinking critically, speaking out and doing community organizing has come from my family. An incident not too long ago reminded me of that. During a particular trial proceeding, police were forced to disclose information that revealed they were keeping a police "intelligence" list of all the Black people in Toronto who had been actively speaking out and organizing against police brutality. My father, who is a civil rights lawyer, and my sister were on the list. I've seen this list, and it's quite hilarious. It had information like the make and licence plate number of my dad's car, his date of birth, and so on. Under my sister's name, it said: "Is being groomed by father to be a leader." At first I thought it was ridiculous, but then I realized it was true. It's true in the sense that, as in many Black families, we children took our strength, our example of living decently and fighting back from our parents and aunts and grannies, not from white male movie actors playing vigilante. We've formed action groups and done political work with other families and community people. I learned a lot through organizing forums and Freedomrides. I can remember going to political meetings and demonstrations on a range of things from immigration to anti-nukes from the time I was small. And this police thing just reminded me that we do have power when we come together. I mean, what were the police scared of? What crime did the people on this list commit? They just spoke up against wrong-doing.

JR: The whole process of being willing to take a risk is also crucial to leadership. I have always said that if you move, you're a target. But a lot of people stop being willing to take risks once they

are in a leadership role, and this happens particularly to politicians. This is a major downfall of the NDP both federally and
provincially. They play it too safe, because they think they will be
marginalized by the mainstream media. Then they get marginalized anyway because no one sees the difference between them and
the other parties. People want to make changes and they get into
politics because they want to make changes. And then, once
they're in any kind of position of power, all that becomes important to them is staying there.

KR: I think this is one reason a lot of people on the Left are
unwilling to do electoral work. Some don't even vote. You know
the old saying: "No matter who you vote for, the government
always gets in." I'll always vote because it's my duty but also
because women and African people all over the world fought so
hard, and some died, to win the right to vote. Now we just need
something to vote for. It's only been eight years since I reached
voting age, but already I'm weary of all the political betrayal in
government. I don't think we live in a real democracy. The vast
majority of people said we didn't want free trade, but we were
ignored. Eighty per cent said no to the Goods and Services Tax,
so Mulroney changed the rules, appointed a few more
Conservatives to an unelected Senate and passed it anyway. The
Liberals came in with a clear mandate to get rid of the GST and
create jobs, and then they turned around and did neither. Instead,
they've gone further in carrying out the kinds of policies
Canadians rejected. The distinctions between the political parties
are blurring. All we have now is gradations of Right.

When Bob Rae was premier in Ontario, he broke promises too.
Many progressive people feel the NDP is straying from its leftist
roots. I've spoken to grassroots movement people who've really
had it with party politics.

JR: But I think the solution has to be to reform the democratic system, not to ignore it. We live in a parliamentary democracy, however imperfect it might be. If there is no Left presence in Parliament, there is no Left presence in political discourse. Just look at what has happened since the NDP took so few seats in the 1993 federal election. Up until the re-election of the NDP under Glen Clark in B.C., the media had itself convinced that the Left was dead.

I think the most significant weakness of the Left in Canada is its failure to understand how to work in electoral politics. Social movements are non-partisan. They share much of the program of the NDP, and no doubt many of their members vote NDP. But they don't support the NDP electorally, and they don't try and transform the nature of the party.

I think what we need to do is to build a movement and a political party simultaneously. And even when that political party takes power, you maintain the political movement, because the political movements are needed to keep the political party honest. One of the reasons why both the Ontario and the B.C. NDP have been so strong on women's issues is that women inside the party were active in the women's movement. Of course, the relationship between the labour movement and the NDP is even closer, but that's mainly at the top. There is a reason why the Right began its public campaign with a fight against "special interest groups." They recognized that the strength of social movements in Canada was a major barrier for them to overcome.

But there's an aversion to electoral politics among a lot of people in the social movements. I remember going to a socialist feminist conference about women and the state in the early eighties. I sat through a two-hour panel in which no one talked about electoral politics, no one. When I resigned as spokesperson for the Ontario Coalition for Abortion Clinics in 1987 to run as a provincial NDP candidate, not a single OCAC activist worked on my campaign.

KR: I'm equivocal about what party politics can do for disadvantaged people, since so much of it seems to be about just staying in power, breaking promises and kowtowing to a big-business agenda. But when I speak to women's groups, I say that we should have 52 per cent representation in Parliament and in every level of government as a basic issue of fairness and democracy. I don't have much faith that we can do anything interesting in electoral politics unless we have a critical number of women in power. I used to say, "Oh, we don't need to enter party politics; look how much the grassroots women's movement has achieved without very many women in government." But the counterargument is that whatever we struggle for on the outside, whether it's funding for women's shelters or legal reform, we can't succeed in obtaining it unless government acts. And we certainly know that while government can't give us everything, they can definitely make life worse for us by bringing in bad laws. So it is important for women to be there. I've also thought, "My god, what would have happened if Elijah Harper hadn't been an MLA in Manitoba to hold up the eagle feather and put a halt to the Meech Lake Accord?"

JR: There's no question that representation of women and minorities in Parliament is important. At the federal level, we have seen the defeat of the abortion law and increased attention to violence against women because of the action of women in all the political parties. Pat Carney, whom I disagree with on almost everything, ruined her career in Mulroney's government by voting against recriminalizing abortion. I wouldn't vote for Pat Carney if my life depended on it, but in the end her courage defeated the abortion law.

On the other hand, just getting more women and more minorities involved in politics does not deal with the fundamental problem. How are the patriarchal, top-down, Machiavellian methods of political parties going to change? It's hard enough to change the organizational culture in groups like NAC, where there is not as much power at stake. But it's also true that if women of colour had not gone into NAC to fight for change, it wouldn't have happened.

KR: Getting more women and people of colour in *does* change patriarchal politics, because to have real participation you're going to have to change the rules and eliminate barriers. It's tough for women to balance family life and a political career. And party politics is also deeply classist; you have to raise thousands of dollars to run a campaign. So changes would have to be made to address all these things. When you get enough people with different life experiences, it does have an impact, although you can't stop there.

It's tough to win a nomination when the party still thinks women and people of colour are less likely to get elected. I know of one case where a South Asian woman was running against a white man for the provincial Liberal Party nomination. The riding association actually changed the rules so that this man could sign up more members past the usual deadline. He won the nomination only because the riding association bent the rules.

JR: When I ran for the federal NDP nomination in Scarborough West in 1988, even though almost everyone believed I was the better candidate, many people on the riding executive supported my male opponent, because he had run several times before and "deserved another chance at it." Systemic discrimination against women in politics takes many forms. But without a stronger movement both inside and outside political parties to challenge discrimination and top-down functioning, nothing will change.

KR: I think more good leftists might be encouraged to go into politics if they didn't see integrity being punished. Even if you go in as a feminist, you still have to obey the party line no matter what. That's one reason the Feminist Party of Canada was formed in the late 1970s, although it never got off the ground.

Zanana Akande's experience is a really good example of what can happen to someone who enters politics. She was an NDP MPP, but what happened to her could have happened in any of the political parties. Here she was in 1990, the first Black woman elected to the Ontario legislature, the first Black woman cabinet minister. She had an impressive record of community service. An allegation was made that she had improperly raised the rent on a duplex she owned and had had renovations done on. She stepped down while the matter was being investigated, and she was subsequently cleared, but Bob Rae did not defend her or support her or invite her back into cabinet. Yet he defended another minister who admitted to having lied about something important. Akande was outspoken. She said unpopular things. She was a strong voice for the Black community, and she helped bring in things like Jobs Ontario Youth, employment equity and anti-racist education. But she paid a price, and she was called "emotional." She resigned before completing her term. In an interview with *Pride* magazine, she was quoted as saying, "I'm too determined and idealistic to settle for peace at the price of my community and their needs. I'm leaving government, not politics."

JR: Politics is dirty. There's nothing more patriarchal than a political party. Some of our most effective women leaders have found it impossible to function in political parties. Doris Anderson and Maude Barlow both gave up trying to change the Liberal Party of Canada from the inside. Rosemary Brown left politics after running for the NDP federal leadership.

If you are critical, and especially if you organize for change, you get labelled a troublemaker, and they don't value your contribution. The leadership of the NDP, whether federally or provincially, never saw me as a valuable asset to the party, despite my high profile, because I was often critical of their policies.

An individual can often be more effective outside a political party, precisely because of the patriarchal and hierarchical nature of the parliamentary system. What matters there are the leaders and the cabinet. Backbench MPs have very little influence. In that 1988 federal nomination fight, I lost by twenty-two votes. If I had won the party nomination, I probably would have won the seat, because I would have run against Liberal Tom Wappel. It would have been World War III, between pro-choice and anti-choice, and I would have gone to Parliament. But where would I have been more effective from 1989 to 1993—as an NDP backbencher or as president of NAC? There's no question I was more effective as president of NAC. So that's the problem.

Part of the solution has to be changes to the parliamentary and electoral systems, and up until now the Right has had more to say about this. When I spoke at the federal NDP policy convention in 1994, I told the party that they had to become more accountable and to support more direct democracy, like referendums. They've got to run on a platform they can implement, and then implement it no matter what. In Britain, they have a system where members have to vote with the government on election platform issues. On everything else, backbenchers can disagree. And in the House of Commons there, backbenchers attack the government with as much ferocity as opposition members do.

Another thing that's absolutely key is proportional representation. Our electoral system is not democratic, because you can win without a majority or even with fewer votes than another party, since it's based on how many ridings you win. It's an undemocratic system. It would also be a lot easier to start a new party if you had proportional representation, because then if you had a certain percentage of the vote, depending on what the minimum was, you'd get a seat. And then you'd be able to show your stuff. Studies in Europe indicate that countries with proportional representation in elections tend to elect a higher proportion of women.

In the debate about the elected Senate in 1992, the constitutional conference on the issue adopted the recommendation that proportional representation be used as a means of electing the Senate. Of course the premiers put the kibosh on it, because so many of them rely on our first-past-the-post system for their power.

KR: I think proportional representation is more democratic, but it doesn't necessarily guarantee that 50 per cent women will get elected. Italy has proportional representation but only 12 to 15 per cent elected women. The other thing is that we would have to build a serious and vigorous campaign to get the system to change, and most of the politically aware women I've talked to roll their eyes at the mere mention of party politics. During the last federal election, I worked with some other women to put on a forum with women candidates from all the different parties, and only a sprinkling of women showed up to listen to the candidates or ask questions. It's a paradox: we've got high dissatisfaction but near zero willingness to do anything about it. Something's got to give. If we don't change the system or do something pro-active, we might have to wait for decades to achieve gender parity, or lose all hope that progressive renewal is possible. I read somewhere that if we continue at the current rate it will take 520 years before women achieve parity in governments worldwide.

The Committee for '94, started in the mid-eighties, was a non-partisan group of women who wanted to see 50 per cent women elected by 1994. It seems reasonable to think that with some hard work over ten years that could have been achieved, but here we are today with eight men to every two women in Parliament. It seems that this is one area where women will have to work across party lines. In 1978 my parents helped found a group called the Movement for Minority Electors, and their approach was to support people of colour wanting to run for office, regardless of party affiliation.

JR: Yes, the Committee for '94 did not exactly achieve its goal. To be most effective, proportional representation has to be combined with quotas, the dreaded "q" word. In Norway, parties were legally required to put at least 40 per cent women on their electoral lists, and the result was dramatic. But even without quotas, proportional representation does result in more women being elected than the current system.

KR: One suggestion I've heard is to expand the ridings and have parties run man/woman teams. So then when people vote for a party they automatically vote for a man and a woman.

JR: But with the move to the Right, any form of affirmative action is out of favour. There was barely a ripple when the Ontario Tories put all white men on the committee looking at employment equity. There were more powerful and influential women in Mulroney's cabinet than there are in Chrétien's. I support any policy that promotes better representation in all political parties, but I don't always vote on that basis. I have always voted NDP. I might be able to vote for a Liberal if she was a strong feminist, but I would never vote Tory or Reform. But even in the NDP I have not always supported women leadership candidates if another candidate reflected my political positions better. So I guess what I am saying is that while representation is important, it is not my only consideration in politics.

KR: We shouldn't reject the idea of having more women in Parliament because some of them might be conservative. If we demand that all women politicians be feminist and run on the NDP ticket then we still won't achieve gender parity, because obviously not everyone will vote NDP. I don't support Kim Campbell's politics, but I think it is good that she was prime minister because it represented a huge advance over the time when women in Canada weren't considered "persons" for the purpose of holding a seat in the Senate.

Riding to riding the situation is not so cut and dried because our system is complex and, depending on the situation, you have a number of competing interests when you go to the ballot box. I don't think it's good to be extremist. If my *life* depended on it I would vote for Pat Carney. On some issue of grave importance to me, I would cross party lines.

A Black Conservative recently ran here for office in a by-election. The party's platform provincially was to scrap employment equity, but municipally this man lobbied people to get more diverse representation among firefighters. In the provincial election in my riding we had to choose between four men: a white Liberal whose race politics I had doubts about, an NDPer who had voted against same-sex spousal benefits, a Progressive Conservative who is Black, and an independent with good politics who didn't have a hope in hell of winning. It's not absolutely clear to me in that situation that I should vote NDP.

Since we're so poorly represented, voting for a woman or a person of colour to achieve fairer representation might be legitimate. It's like picking juries: you don't know what the person's politics are, but it makes sense not to have an all-male jury panel in a rape case because there is something to be said for life experience. Take Lincoln Alexander, the first and to date the only Black federal cabinet minister, under Joe Clark. The first Black elected to federal parliament, in 1968. He is a Conservative, but he spoke out to stop the unfair deportation of seven Jamaican domestics in 1978. Ellen Fairclough, a Conservative minister of immigration in the sixties, brought in new rules to allow Black people to immigrate to Canada as independents. Jean Augustine, a Liberal, got Black History Month officially recognized in Canada.

When you get right down to it, *all* parties want one thing: to stay in power. It's good to have a few allies in government, but most politicians just react to the demands of whoever they think is most powerful. An article in *Ms* reported that the Swedish government is 41 per cent women. Fifty per cent of the cabinet is women. But because Sweden had a prolonged recession and a big deficit, the male finance minister, who wields the most power, was ordering harsh cuts. So this record number of women was presiding over the slashing of social spending. As one Swede said, it is a "fantastic symbol for the world, but for the women in Parliament it is a shock because they feel no power." Power is still in the hands of globalized financial institutions. But I still think numbers *are* important. Just because government is under pressure from business doesn't mean you give up on government. It means you use grassroots pressure to change things.

JR: Because of all the problems with political parties and the parliamentary system itself, not to mention global capitalism, a lot of people argue that we should build coalitions among the social movements that can pressure all the political parties to bring in progressive measures. I think this is the wrong approach. Coalition politics are important, but they're not a substitute for party politics. I think the Swedish example shows that we have to look at some models in Latin America for political parties that combine the characteristics of social movements and parties and that base themselves on the mobilization of the people, and not on the existing institutions of political power. The Brazilian Workers Party is a good example.

KR: We've never seen a political party mobilize people. In Canada, it's not realistic to think that a government is going to also be down there in the streets mobilizing people to do this, that or the other.

JR: But that's exactly what a left-wing government has to do. And it has to start by recognizing the conflicting interests in society. The business class is waging war against workers' rights and quality of life. And a party that represents working people has to give up the idea that they can govern by being nicey-nice to Bay Street. If our political culture won't support government-backed mobilizations, then a left-wing political party can use referendums to mobilize the population on key issues. So, for example, instead of backing off on public auto insurance, which they had promised, the NDP under Bob Rae could have had a referendum on public auto insurance and gotten what I think would have been an 85 per cent vote in favour. A socialist party has to understand its reliance on the mass movement, and the people who are active in social movements have to get active in the party.

KR: But once in power, the conflict the government usually faces is between keeping the promises it made and staying in power. It's our job to create the climate to get government to respond to our needs. I can't think of a single piece of progressive legislation or program that a political party has brought in without a lot of pressure from activists. We have to remember that no matter what party is in power. If you're a strong grassroots movement and you have a Conservative government then you know you have to mobilize, but when the NDP was in power in Ontario, progressive people kind of gave up. We said, "Okay, we elected the NDP, now let them do it." And we just abandoned the political terrain on many levels. For their part, people inside the government, even those who had been active in social movements before, said, "Leave us alone. We can handle it now."

JR: That was a big mistake. Because if we'd mobilized ourselves to push them, it would have helped them as well as us. But even when there was a major division between the NDP and the labour movement, on the social contract, the unions most opposed to the Rae government decided to sit out the election rather than deciding to organize inside the NDP or perhaps even challenge Rae's leadership.

I'm not saying give up the social movements—absolutely not—but we have to put our minds to either transforming the NDP or building a new political party based on egalitarian principles. And we have to deal with the issue of political power. We can't just see ourselves as pressure groups.

10

From the Bottom Up

BUILDING FOR CHANGE

KR: Things are so hard-line with this new breed of right-wingers governing the land. I hope this will radicalize people faster and more than it hardens us. Homeless men freeze to death on the streets in winter and women with children who've had their welfare cheques cut are being evicted from their apartments. Governmental agencies want to respond with a warm blanket program and hostels instead of housing. The stage seems set for more strikes and violent confrontations with the police.

JR: People forget that when we had demonstrations in the sixties, we had cops with clubs riding on horses through them beating people over the head. That was in the streets of Toronto, Vancouver and Montreal. It wasn't as bad as in the States; nobody got killed, nobody got shot. But that was the level of polarization. And certainly in Ontario and Atlantic Canada, we are dealing with a level of political and social polarization we have not seen since then.

KR: This is the backdrop as we reevaluate our beliefs and our struggles. I think we're tired of hearing, "Stop the cuts, stop the cuts." There have been people putting out different alternatives, like a shorter work week, a national child-care program, and so on, for years. We have to ask ourselves why these alternatives aren't being explored and how it is that people on the Left are not bringing forth our ideas in a way that captures people's imaginations. We need to develop our different strategies with some sense of creativity and joy. It's depressing to come down to the legislature for another mock funeral mourning the death of our social programs. We need to find ways to sustain ourselves emotionally, to anchor ourselves in optimism, because this is going to be a long struggle. Many of us have trouble believing that we can turn back the whole monetarist right-wing agenda. I think a lot of people see it as a global phenomena that is way out of our hands, too big. So we have to convince people that they actually do have power. We can do that partly by recalling our past victories and by making sure that what we do now is effective.

JR: The problems we face are global in nature, and therefore the solutions have to be global too. There are alternatives that can be pursued at a national level, and we have to fight for those. But we also have to work with others around the world to develop alternatives. That's why I think one of the most important things that Sunera Thobani accomplished as president of NAC was to get NAC involved in the global women's movement. One thing I became more aware of in Huairou was how much we can learn from what people in the South are doing. And there are a few global organizing efforts going on right now.

KR: A great model for coalition that we could look to is a group called CAFRA, the Caribbean Association for Feminist Research and Action, that started about ten years ago. They've brought together women academics and activists, trade unionists and NGO groups from across the entire Caribbean region to share ideas about how to develop real alternatives to the specific problems women face in confronting structural adjustment programs. They've managed to bring together women from many different sectors, including even political parties, to do ground-breaking research on how women are affected in the free trade zones and to organize protests against that exploitation. What I'm most impressed with is how they have broken down class barriers and succeeded in melding theory, research and action.

One of the most dynamic international protest movements was the worldwide struggle to end apartheid in South Africa. It was ordinary people who put pressure on their governments to isolate the apartheid regime. It was students and community leaders who forced corporations to divest their holdings in South African companies. It was the international community responding to the call of Black South Africans to boycott that country on every level— that combined external and internal pressure—that brought apartheid down. Right now there's a call to boycott Shell Oil for their role in propping up the regime in Nigeria, where Ken Saro-Wiwa and other political dissidents were executed. And people have been calling for a boycott of GAP clothing because the company manufactures in countries where workers are poorly paid and working under terrible conditions.

JR: I think the campaign against the GAP was more a protest than a boycott. But it did seem to be effective. As part of that "clean clothes campaign," I wrote a short letter to the GAP expressing my concern, and I got a three-page letter back saying that they believe in fair labour practices and they had had this complaint investigated. It was a very serious response. And I heard later that the campaign did result in some improved conditions for El Salvadoran workers in GAP source plants. So corporations can be subject to pressure, and international campaigns can work. The boycott in response to French nuclear testing is interesting. It was almost spontaneous. I didn't hear anyone call for a boycott of French products, but I know all kinds of people said they wouldn't buy French wine, they wouldn't buy French cheese. People are voting with their feet, their money.

Right now many groups are so busy fighting against the cuts for their very survival that it is difficult to be creative, and it becomes more difficult to have the inevitably divisive discussions that new ideas entail. But we need to continue our resistance to attacks as well as coming up with alternatives.

KR: I'm one of the people who still believes very strongly in demonstrations. I've seen them work. I've seen them do all kinds of incredibly wild, wonderful things. Mass demonstrations toppled the long and brutal regimes of Marcos in the Philippines and Duvalier in Haiti. They've won us human rights. They won us our social safety net in Canada. I'm really encouraged when people come out to demonstrations. We have to make sure that there's visible opposition to what's going on. Sometimes civil disobedience actions can work too, even when they're undertaken on a small scale. One example is a sit-in by students at York University, who were protesting the way security guards were always stopping Black students on campus for no good reason. Students got fed up with this, and they decided to occupy the administration's offices. And from that moment on, things changed. There was an investigation and that kind of activity stopped. The Clayoquot Sound protests on the west coast of B.C., where more than nine hundred people risked their bodies to try to stop this total environmental devastation, commanded world attention. Big companies and the B.C. government were forced to recognize the situation and do something about it. Many different kinds of civil disobedience actions have, if not totally won the situation for whatever group was involved, at least pushed the issue onto centre stage.

JR: Civil disobedience can certainly move an issue to the front burner, but it rarely serves to mobilize large numbers of people. Clayoquot Sound was an exception. Another exception was the opening of illegal abortion clinics in the early eighties. In both cases, the civil disobedience tactic served to catapult an issue into the news and to the front of the political agenda, and also to mobilize a lot of people. But often a civil disobedience action can simply get the issue onto the front page for a day or two.

KR: Well, to work, an action has to be connected to a movement.

JR: For me, building the movement is what's important. I think we've gotten away from building our movements at a grassroots level, and we have to get back to that. That means the hard, slogging work of organizing. I guess the most successful grassroots organizing I was ever involved in was the struggle in support of the Morgentaler clinic in Toronto. There were very similar movements organized in Montreal, Winnipeg and Vancouver. That struggle is a good example, because it shows how much more effective it is to organize for something positive rather than just organizing against something. In 1980, a number of women's health workers in Toronto were concerned about decreasing access to abortion across the province. They decided to find doctors who would be willing to open a free-standing abortion clinic in Toronto, like the one Dr. Morgentaler had opened in Montreal. To make a long story short, it was finally Henry Morgentaler himself who opened the clinic, but over a period of almost eight years, from the first meeting of the Ontario Coalition for Abortion Clinics to the Supreme Court decision striking down the abortion law, we were able to organize a huge mass movement in support of legalizing abortion. It took the form of a movement in support of the clinic itself, and people were mobilized when the state tried to close the clinic through the courts or when the anti-choice faction tried to close the clinic on the streets. It was a conscious campaign that started with getting support for opening the clinic from organizations like the Ontario Federation of Labour, then went through organizing an escort service to protect patients from police intimidation in the early days and anti-choice intimidation later on, to responding publicly to all government and church initiatives, to organizing mass demonstrations. OCAC was a new group, but we worked in concert with CARAL, the Canadian Abortion Rights Action League, which had been lobbying and educating on abortion for a long time. To CARAL's credit, they worked with the new group even though they often had differences with us.

One of the strengths of a visible movement, like the pro-choice movement in the 1980s, is that people begin to identify with your struggle, whether or not they have ever had a direct role in it. For example, a few months after the Morgentaler clinic finally opened, the police announced to the media that an immigrant woman had complained to them that she was abused at the clinic and forced to have an abortion after she changed her mind. We knew this was not true, but it was our word against the chief of police's. Within twenty-four hours, a number of people—the taxi driver who had driven the woman home and said she was perfectly happy until the police confronted her; a hospital worker who was there when the woman arrived at emergency with the police; and an immigration officer who knew that the woman was in Canada illegally and that the police had probably threatened her with deportation—had all called the clinic with their information. That was the moment I knew we were going to win the struggle. This kind of multifaceted campaign to achieve a particular goal is rare now and perhaps harder to organize in today's climate. You've participated in mobilizing people in the Embarrass Harris campaign. How does that compare?

KR: Well, when Mike Harris first got elected, I would be on the subway or in a store or something, and total strangers would come up to me and start talking about politics because they saw me wearing an anti-Harris button. There is shock and anger and insecurity as more people lose their jobs or can't get jobs because of the cutbacks. There have been meetings and demonstrations and the historic OPSEU (Ontario Public Service Employees Union) strike this year, where for the first time more than 60,000 public servants walked out. But we don't yet have a movement in the sense of a groundswell of opposition from the public demanding change. The problem today, with the Ontario government bringing down omnibus bills and the federal government attacking so many things in one bill, as they did with the CHST, is that they're hitting us on many different sides at once. I think people get depressed when these things happen, and you see them withdrawing and feeling fearful. The only way I know of to get over this fear is to take action.

Embarrass Harris started when a few of us met at a NAC conference, days after the Ontario election, and heard Anne McGrath of Alberta talk about how harsh the cutbacks were there, how even more right-wing the province had become. That made us snap into action. So for two weeks, a small group of people got

together and planned a massive demo tied to the opening of the
Ontario legislature. We didn't have a lot of long meetings with
representatives of different groups. There was a core group of
young people who had worked on a lot of different campaigns and
who knew how to organize. We had a couple of meetings where
we got the basic information out and then people went off into
their own groups and did the organizing. In a really short time we
had more than 2,000 people out at Queen's Park. And two months
later, more than 7,000 came out for the Throne Speech demo.

What attracted me to Embarrass Harris was that the people in
it were ready and willing to act. We would be where the Tories
were and ruin their events. We'd engage the media with good
clear graphics and short punchy slogans on our signs, and we
have a sense of timing. For example, when Mike Harris got back
from a junket in Asia and was meeting with businessmen, he held
a press conference. Two Embarrass Harris members walked in
and right in front of him unfurled a huge red flag that said, "Nix
26." Bill 26 is an omnibus bill that concentrates a lot of power into
the government's hands.

JR: Those are similar to the kinds of tactics Greenpeace has used
over the years to draw attention to their issues. That approach
does work, but my concern is that inevitably only a small elite
group is involved. So while it raises the issue in the media, I don't
really think it winds up making people feel empowered.

KR: The point is that it's not either/or; it's both/and. You do the
big *and* the small actions. I have no problem talking about ideas
and negotiating with different groups, because I think it's essential to have mediation skills and coalition politics. But I have to
say that I'm more excited by direct action groups than by sitting

in large meetings with people who are arguing over trivial points. You can have a lot of people at a meeting, but when it comes down to who actually does the work, it's usually only a small group of people anyway. Smaller groups can do concrete direct actions, but the question is whether they can sustain political action over a long period of time. Small groups tend to have a short life span.

JR: That's interesting, because the Ontario Coalition for Abortion Clinics, which was also a direct action group in a lot of ways, began as a coalition of groups and ended up as a committee of individuals who worked in coalition with other groups on specific occasions. So maybe what we are saying here is that long-term, formal coalitions are not necessarily a good thing. My experience in the Action Canada Network, for example, is that it worked well when it had a single focus, the Canada/U.S. Free Trade Agreement. But when that fight was over and the focus was diluted, the group became a lot less effective. Maybe we need coalitions to come together for specific actions or campaigns, like the Women's March against Poverty, and then dissolve until the next action. And maybe we need to leave space for small direct action groups to initiate action and stimulate the larger, more bureaucratic groups to act.

KR: I think we could learn a lot about coalition work from the Fédération des femmes du Québec's Bread and Roses women's march that happened in 1995. The Fédération worked with about twenty different women's organizations across Quebec over a two-year period. They had a plan, and they came up with nine very clear demands on the government to improve women's lives, like raising the minimum wage, targeting job training for women, and so on. They presented the Quebec government with these demands. And then they used their march and rally not just as a protest but as a tool to apply pressure on the politicians to have their demands met. By marching through small towns over ten days on their way to Quebec City, they raised awareness and developed a strong network of supporters in all of these communities.

JR: That march took a very different approach to social issues in Quebec and put tremendous pressure on the Parti Québécois to adopt a more compassionate stance towards poverty. The organizers worked on lobbying the government at the same time as they organized women at a grassroots level. To me their success came from the combination of their demands and the power of hundreds of women marching together through towns and villages all the way from Montreal to Quebec City to say, "We should not have poverty among women and children in Quebec. It is not necessary, and here are some ways we can eliminate it." This was a powerful and visible alternative to the "blame the poor" message we get from right-wing politicians. I think the NAC/CLC women's march had a similar impact. Not only did thousands of new women get involved, but within days after the march ended, Prime Minister Chrétien talked about eliminating poverty as a priority for the imminent First Ministers' conference.

KR: We are addicted to instant gratification in this society, but changing power relations takes a long time. We can't just say, oh well, we've had four demonstrations and nothing changed, so let's give up. I think of the civil rights movement in the States. There you had Black people boycotting the transit system because there was discriminatory treatment—"you have to sit in the back" and all that kind of stuff. And people actually walked, they did everything else but take the bus for 381 days. With that determination, that commitment, they practically bankrupted the transit system, and that was when change really happened. We too have to stand fast and not give up.

JR: We also have to think of more creative ways to organize. In the sixties and seventies, we didn't focus all our energy on the state; we went after corporations, we protested cultural institutions. For example, the first action of the women's movement in the U.S. was against the Miss America beauty pageant. The beginning of the fight for affirmative action in Canada was directed at getting women hired into Stelco. The environmental movement targets corporations a lot. I think we have to do that kind of thing more. After all, the corporations are the real villains here.

KR: Yes, and the banks.

JR: The banks and other multinational corporations. They're sensitive to public pressure. Just look at that Bank of Montreal ad campaign with people holding picket signs saying things like, "Banks are only for rich people." God, it's weird living in the nineties. They co-opt protest before it even happens. Anyway, I think we've concentrated way too much on government partly because we've had some success. Obviously government's very important, but there are other institutions in society that need to change and become more accountable too.

KR: But many people seem convinced that lobbying the government is *the* thing to do.

JR: Well, lobbying is an important aspect of any campaign. But I think too many groups rely on having an inside track with this bureaucrat or that minister, and it creates a lot of cautiousness.

Some groups lobby the same way businesses lobby. But business lobbies have power and influence because of their money and connections. Social change groups only have the power of their ability to mobilize public opinion. There's a myth that if you have the right connections with such and such a bureaucrat or so and so a minister you can convince them to take up your issue. Sometimes the interests of your constituency can coincide with the interests of the government or the minister and then lobbying can work, like around the rape law with Kim Campbell. But not often.

In all my years in the women's movement, the only thing I have ever seen achieved primarily by lobbying was the defeat in the Senate of Bill C-43, the abortion bill. I made the presentation to the Senate on behalf of NAC, and it was the first time I ever felt a parliamentary committee was actually listening to what I said. The Senate was split down the middle on the issue and it was a free vote, so they were interested in the argument. But in all my experience, and this is true with the NDP, the Liberals and the Tories, that is the only time I ever felt lobbying made a major difference.

I think any successful campaign has to have a combination of tactics. Sometimes one group will focus on lobbying and another will focus on street demonstrations, but any campaign has to have a combination.

KR: That was true in the anti-apartheid movement here. People demanded the economic boycotts. But also there were teach-ins, and artists and writers held cultural events. Lawyers tried to bring a court injunction to stop the South African ambassador from speaking at the University of Toronto. And musicians held concerts against apartheid. The African National Congress opened branch offices worldwide. The whole struggle went beyond just your usual handing out of pamphlets and demonstrations,

although we had a lot of those. During the civil rights movements people organized Freedomrides. What happened there was
that white and Black Freedomriders travelled together by bus to
integrate rest stops throughout the U.S. My family took that
example and, with other community organizers, we adapted it to
fight apartheid. We organized busloads of people from different
parts of Ontario and Quebec to travel in protest to Ottawa to get
the government to break diplomatic ties with South Africa. The
great thing about the Freedomrides was that people of all different
backgrounds and levels of awareness used the four or five hours
of both ways on the bus to get to know each other and to debate
issues and talk about racism in Canada. And to sing. We built
community right there on the bus. I saw people who had never been
on a protest in their lives before change through the process. I saw
people's consciousness change. As the momentum builds, people
find themselves using every means available to organize.

JR: We can't talk about organizing without talking about the
Internet. Promoters of the Internet say it is empowering because
it is interactive. They say it will democratize the media. I doubt it.
But I do think it can be a fantastic organizing tool. NAC couldn't
have run our referendum campaign in 1992 without e-mail. Every
night I could put debating points or questions and answers out on
the e-mail, and other spokespeople across the country would have
instant access. Now, with the World Wide Web, you can provide
an incredible amount of information to large numbers of people.
Embarrass Harris has a terrific web site. I used it the other day
and got documents from the Ontario Federation of Labour listing
the cuts and other attacks by the Harris government.

KR: The Internet is a great resource for small groups who
can't afford researchers. It's being used really effectively by rural

communities. It's a powerful resource for learning more about the world, too, because what we know about what is going on in Central and South America, Africa and Asia is very limited.

JR: Yes, you can actually access information directly from a liberation movement in a particular country and not get it filtered through the mainstream media. On the international level, it is really amazing. The Zapatistas in Mexico have a home page with all these statements from Sub-Commandante Marcos translated into English.

KR: The sheer volume of information on the Internet can be overwhelming, though. Some people argue that technology depersonalizes the movement and reinforces physical isolation or detachment from people around you. And even though revolutionary groups are on the net, the technology is still not available to poor people.

JR: The Internet is a good tool, but it's not a substitute for organizing with people. The idea of virtual community is in my view a crock. People sitting at their computer screens are not a community, they are individuals. Participating in an Internet debate is not the same thing as participating in a live discussion, and nothing on the Internet even approaches the experience or the impact of a mass demonstration.

KR: I've talked to people who have been involved in many different movements but today they feel isolated and paralyzed. Why aren't we seeing mass resistance to the attacks? We see CEOs making millions of dollars while people are put out of work. We see governments gutting our social programs.

JR: Well, I think we're in a period of transition now. Social democracy has failed, communism has failed, and people around the world are looking for a new model of social justice. A wise friend of mine once pointed out to me when I was having a very hard time in my life that the myth of wandering after a moment of crisis is a myth that's universal. Jesus and Moses, for example, both spent a long time wandering in the desert. A central part of the myth is that a period of confusion often precedes a moment of revelation. I think we're in the desert now, and it's tough. But I believe that a new movement is in formation. At the same time as some people are tying themselves in theoretical knots and others are subsumed by the backlash, many others are organizing and standing up for the first time.

KR: In Canada, we tend to be polite. There's a kind of culture of deference that we have to overcome. At times we've seen some major cross-Canada mobilizing: the abortion caravan of 1970, the On to Ottawa trek, the recent Women's March against Poverty. We had a Black Panther movement in Nova Scotia in the sixties, and more and more we see people of the First Nations defending their land and reclaiming their rights. You talked earlier about the importance of building the movement, and I think this is the direction we need to head in. A movement is more than just a few scattered protests, occasional faxing or a petition here and there. A movement develops analysis. It has a vision and a theory that form the basis for both long-term and short-term action.

JR: Yes, I think we need to combine the strengths of all the various social movements. The labour movement brings the understanding of organizing those without power to confront the powerful, the idea of a school of tiny fish being able to combat the big fish that is trying to eat them. The women's movement brings the struggle to achieve equality, the fight against the domination of any one group, whether men over women, white over Black, or employer over worker. The gay and lesbian rights movement has shown us the strength of community in the face of adversity. The environmental movement insists on us seeing ourselves as part of an ecosystem and learning ways to nurture the Earth rather than destroy it. The anti-racist movement has taught us about resisting the marginalization of whole groups of people and about the way we are all hurt by divide-and-conquer strategies. The movements that used non-violent civil disobedience taught us the power of non-cooperation with violence and injustice. Our social movements have an extraordinary richness and depth if we can harness the best of them and learn from each other. We started to do that with coalitions, but coalitions are too administrative. What we need is a movement of movements.

KR: We are beginning to witness different movements intersecting and taking inspiration from each other. I saw this developing in the Pan-African movement at the seventh Pan-African Congress in Uganda in 1994. Pan-Africanism is a philosophy and a political movement to create solidarity among people of African descent all over the world so that we can support each other's struggles for freedom and self-determination. Over time Pan-Africanists have focussed on things like demanding reparations for slavery and supporting national liberation struggles. At the 1994 congress, for the first time women played a central role in defining the agenda of this movement. Women argued that it would be the strength of African women's liberation movements organizing marginalized women and developing a gender analysis, combined with the more traditional Pan-African demands, that would revitalize the movement. Supporting struggles for equality between men and women would empower communities to fight back against structural adjustment programs, and so on. It's seeing that supporting each other in our different struggles makes us more powerful as allies in our common struggles.

JR: You can see it in South Africa, too, where women were instrumental in ensuring that gay and lesbian rights were protected in the South African constitution. In the Canadian Women's March against Poverty, the strengths of the women's movement and the labour movement joined to become more than the sum of their parts. And that march was inspired by the Quebec women's march, which took its inspiration from the civil rights marches of the sixties.

KR: The power of these movements working together is untold. It's up to progressive people to nurture a climate in which larger movements for justice can emerge. We do that by organizing. We do it by building community, involving new people. We do it by giving expression to our longings for change. I think as we build cultures of resistance to the Right, a more just system will come in answer to our struggles.

ACKNOWLEDGEMENTS

First, we both want to thank Judy's nephew, Lucas. We woke him up every Sunday morning for a year and he never complained. We didn't use his title for the book, "Love in the Time of Cutbacks," but we liked it best.

Our deepest appreciation to Barbara Pulling, our editor, who worked with us from conception to conclusion. Neither of us understood before how important an editor is to the production of a book. Without Barbara's guiding hand, it is doubtful our book would have been written, and it is certain it would never have been read. Thanks too go to Tara Colley-Cleveland and Susan Littleton, who typed the transcripts of our conversations and even added their own voices once or twice.

We both talked to many women about this book, some of whom are quoted and some of whom are not. We thank them all for their insight and generous assistance. The women and men whose lives and work have inspired each of us must also be acknowledged, among them the poet Audre Lorde, to whose memory we have dedicated this book. Audre's life and writing have profoundly educated us both.

Kiké: Hetty, Charles, Sunset and Dawn are the loving family that sustains and inspires me. I am grateful for Sunset's additional support. Deep gratitude to Dad for his endless words of wisdom. I am especially thankful to Judy Rebick, whose friendship and generosity have encouraged my growth and whose insight and humour made the process of *Politically Speaking* a pleasure.

Judy: In my very public life, writing this book with Kiké has been a singularly private activity. I thank Kiké for her amazing courage in taking up the challenge of this dialogue, her hard work in making it happen and her extraordinary wisdom. Thank you to the women I have worked with in NAC, who have taught me so much. To Alvin, Glenna, Sue and Gord, who sustain me. And to the young people in my life: Lucas, Kael, Terra, Tara, Julia, Kayla and Ngozi. They give me courage, hope and joy, and they'll get the biggest kick out of seeing their names in a book.

JUDY REBICK is one of Canada's best-known feminists and political commentators. President of the National Action Committee on the Status of Women from 1990 to 1993, she is also a former president of the Ontario NDP Women's Committee and former spokesperson for the Ontario Coalition for Abortion Clinics. She is currently co-host of *Face Off*, CBC Newsworld's nightly debate show.

KIKÉ ROACH is a community organizer and public speaker who has worked with the Black Students Network of McGill University, SHAKTI: Womanist Collective, the Montreal Collective of Black Women, the Women's Coalition for Employment Equity and African Canadian Youth Initiatives. A former executive member of the National Action Committee on the Status of Women, she has led numerous anti-racism workshops and appears frequently as a media spokesperson on social justice issues.